# Phone Calls in English

Sander M. Schroevers

# Contents

## Getting Started and Ending a Conversation  5
- Calling according to plan  6
- After the greeting  9
- I beg your pardon?  18
- Connecting people  20
- Answering the phone  22
- Ending a conversation  22

## Typical Situations and How To Deal with Them  27
- Taking and leaving messages  28
- Appointments  30
- Telephone spelling  38
- Taking down names and numbers  42
- Electronic addresses  45
- Answering machine  49
- Mobile telephones  52

## Special Situations  55
- Conference calls  56
- International trade  68
- Sales and finances  79
- Travel enquiries  83
- A job interview by telephone  87

## Practical Reference — 91
- Intercultural communication — 92
- Pronunciation — 94
- False friends — 98
- Telecommunications terminology — 100
- Translated geographical names — 102
- Key terms: the company — 103
- Linguistic differences: UK – USA — 109
- Telephone sources on the Internet — 114
- Country codes and dialling codes for well-known cities — 116
- Official holidays and translations — 118
- Temperature conversion table — 122
- Weights and measures — 123

- Index — 125

# Introduction

The TaschenGuide *Phone Calls in English* is intended as a guide for people whose profession requires them to make international telephone calls. Although anyone technically can make phone calls, this tends to get a lot more difficult in another language. How to answer a foreign phone call in a correct way, if you're not prepared for it? How to leave messages on an answering machine or a mobile telephone?

Such things can make many people insecure, especially in a foreign language. The telephone situations cover a wide range of business interactions, which are organised into functional sections to provide a quick reference when making real calls. It will certainly help you to make a good first impression.

The material in this TaschenGuide is written to give you the skills you need for effective business phone calls and to build your confidence in a systematic way.

Wishing you every success with that,

*Sander Schroevers, ll.m*

# Getting Started and Ending a Conversation

When calling in another language it is often difficult finding the right words to start or end a conversation.

In this chapter, you will learn,
- how to make a good first impression (page 7),
- how to formulate your opening questions (page 9),
- how to ask for persons (page 12),
- and how to end a call in a friendly way (page 22).

# Calling according to plan

Making phone calls in another language can be difficult at first, especially for someone who doesn't speak the language fluently yet. That is why important business telephone calls should never be made on the spur of the moment. Because telephone conversations tend to be short and you do not have eye contact, it is difficult to adjust what you are saying as you go along. Advance preparation can be a big help.

## Check-list: advance preparation

1 Look up international dialling codes.
2 Decide who the best person is to talk to.
3 Decide who the next best person is to talk to.
4 Decide the objective(s) of the call.
5 Think of specific desired information.
6 Make a list of key points to be covered.
7 Write down what to say in the opening sentences.

**Vocabulary:**
on the spur of the moment: spontan
objective: Zielsetzung

# Beginning a call

When you call someone it is important to observe the following: identify yourself and your company clearly, because there is only one first impression. But also try to make a positive closing, as that is usually best remembered. Always let the caller hang up first. It is helpful to prepare some expressions for the following situations during the start of a telephone conversation:

- how to introduce yourself with your name and company name,
- how to ask for a specific person, if the phone is answered by someone else,
- how to explain the reason for your call, and ask whether your call is convenient,
- how to leave a message in case the person you wish to talk to isn't available.

In English-speaking cultures it is common to exchange a few polite phrases about unimportant or uncontroversial matters at the beginning and ending of a conversation. This is called 'small talk' and considered an important part of building business relationships. For further details please refer to the specific paragraph.

**Vocabulary:**
observe: beachten
desired: erwünscht
elaborate: näher eingehen

## Example

A: Good morning. Tulip Technology. Ali speaking.
B: Hi Ali, this is Jule at Oberbilk Computing
A: Oh, hi Jule. How are you?
B: Good, thanks. Have I rung you at a busy time?
A: No, now is fine. What can I do for you?

A: Hello. Accounts.
B: Hello. It's Czeslawa. Is Albrecht there?
A: No, he isn't. Shall I try someone else for you?
B: No, I think I'd rather leave him a message.
A: Right, one moment. I'm just getting a pen. OK. Go ahead.
B: Well, I need Albrecht to submit an estimate by Thursday.
A: OK, Czeslawa. I'll give him the message. Anything else?
B: No that's it. Thank you very much. Goodbye.

# Telephone scripts

In order to make their call more goal oriented, people often work with so-called telephone scripts. These allow a caller to structure a conversation and think in advance about possible answers and changes of topic. Telephone scripts are best printed in a readable size (13 points or more). Also write down some specific translations, the spelling of a name or website etc. It will lead to telephone calls (in another language) with better results.

## Example

| | | |
|---|---|---|
| | Name and contact details | Mrs. Shizuka Moriwaki<br>51 E.42nd Street, New York<br>+1-212 661 5151 |
| | Own name (in English spelling) | Heiko. That's H for Harry, E for Easy, I for Item, K for King and O for Oliver. |
| | Own (international) telephone number | +49-211-712257 |
| | Opening phrase | My name's Heiko Broschek of Train AG. I'm calling about our next meeting. |
| | Is it convenient? | *No:* shall I call back at 2 PM or 4 PM? |
| | Did you receive my report? | *Yes:* can I ask your opinion?<br>*No:* would you like me to e-mail it to you now? |
| | Ending phrase | Thank you for your time. It has been very nice talking to you again. |

**Vocabulary:**
telephone script: Dialogschema

# After the greeting

Try to identify yourself and your company clearly because there is only one first impression. But also try to make a positive closing, as that is usually best remembered. Always let the caller hang up first. At the beginning of a call there are a number of different ways of clarifying who you are. These follow a similar pattern:

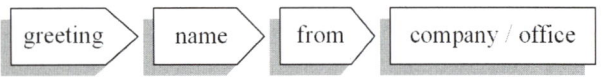

## Introducing yourself

- Good morning. It's Franziska Hauser here, from head office.
- Hello. My name's Andreas Obermaier from sales.
- Good afternoon, this is Chris from Tulip Technology.
- Hi, Jule speaking, from the Düsseldorf office.
- This is Antje. Is that Jack? Speaking.

**Vocabulary:** speaking: am Apparat

> Don't say 'hello' or 'hi', unless you already know a person well. Don't call *yourself* 'Mr'; however, 'Mrs' is fine for women.

## Using first names

In contact with Americans, Australians, New Zealanders or Irish, it is normal to switch quickly to using first names. People from cultures that use family names in combination with Mr and Mrs may feel a bit uneasy perhaps. But the social consequence of not being on first-name terms with a person is the risk of appearing distant or even unfriendly. So simply follow the approach of your conversation partner. It would probably sound exaggerated to suggest saying 'Du', as there is no difference between 'Du' and 'Sie' in English.

## Nicknames

Many Americans or other English-speaking people commonly use nicknames in business contacts. To address them with their full first name could even look somewhat exaggerated. In the same way as names like Maximilian and Gabriele may be shortened to Max and Gabi, the English language shortens first names. Examples of common nicknames are: Harry for Harold, Tony for Anthony, Bob for Robert, Gene for Eugene, Jack for John, Bill for William, Frank for Francis and Ted for Edward. Irish nicknames can also be spelled in Gaelic sometimes (for example: Seán for John, Liam for William).

**Vocabulary:**
be on first-name terms with somebody: duzen
nickname: Spitzname
Gaelic: gälisch

## What's in a name?

In certain countries other words than first and 'last name' may also be used. For instance, in the Republic of Ireland the word 'Christian name' is often used in official papers. Also note that 'first name' may refer to any forename, not just the very first.

| | |
|---|---|
| Given name 🇺🇸 / Forename 🇬🇧 | Vorname |
| First name 🇺🇸 | Vorname |
| Christian name | Vorname (Taufname) |
| Family name | Nachname (Familienname) |
| Surname 🇬🇧 | Nachname (Zuname) |
| Last name / Second name | Nachname |

Most married women (still) adopt their husband's family name. When a woman decides to use both names (e.g. Hillary Rodham Clinton), the second last name (unlike the practice in German-speaking areas) is the husband's family name. However, when two last names are written with a hyphen, this indicates that it is a double last name.

### Asking to speak to someone

When asking to speak to a person it is best to use politer expressions such as: 'could I' or 'I'd like to speak to' instead of a too direct phrasing like 'I want to speak to'.

- Could I speak to Jack Miller please?
- Could you put me through to Mrs Schätzing, the import department, please?
- I should like to speak to Mr. Staebel, please.
- I'd like to speak to the head of the purchasing department, please.
- Can I speak to his secretary / assistant, please?

### Who's calling please?

- Sorry, who's calling / speaking, please?
- I'm sorry, who shall I say is calling?
- Yes, of course. And your name again?
- Sorry, what did you say your name was?
- Are you one of our suppliers?
- What would you like to speak to him / her about?

**Vocabulary:**
phrasing: Formulierung
supplier: Lieferant

## The reason for the call

Whether you get to talk to a person directly, or by way of a secretariat or colleague, it is always important to know how to explain the reason for your telephone call. In the illustration below you can see the normal grammatical arrangement of noun and verb (verb + ing form) after an introductory phrase.

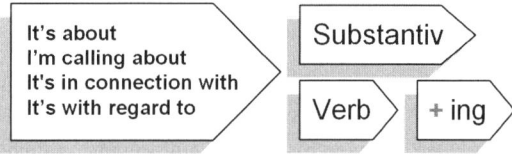

- It's / I'm calling in connection with Friday's conference.
- I'm phoning / ringing about the PowerPoint presentation.
- I'm calling to discuss the conference of next Friday.
- I'm phoning to inform you about the changes.
- It's about placing an order.
- The reason I'm phoning is Friday's conference.

### Is it convenient?

To check if the person who answers the phone has time to talk can be done with the following phrases:

- Are you busy right now?
- Do you have a sec / second?
- Is this a good moment to talk?
- Have I rung you at a bad moment, Christa?
- Can we talk now or perhaps later?
- What time do you want me to call you back?
- Do you mind calling back this afternoon?
- Sorry, can you call again later?

## Small talk

Small talk is used in English-speaking cultures, to influence conversations in a positive way. Small talk is very functional to introduce or end a conversation, with a few phrases about friendly and risk-free topics. Please note that the question 'How do you do?' is best answered with 'How do you do?' or 'I'm fine, thank you. How are you?'. Below are some more phrases to begin or end a call:

- It's ages since we spoke.
- We haven't spoken since the Frankfurt Book Fair.
- How is business for you?
- So how have you been?
- So how old are the kids now?

- When are you coming to Europe?
- We must really speak again soon.
- I look forward to hearing from you again.

## Getting past the secretary

One cannot always reach a contact directly, and sometimes it might even be necessary to 'get past the secretary'. If it comes to that, it is always good to have one or two phrases prepared that quickly explain the connection or reason for the call.

- Well, it's a bit technical / complicated. Can I have a quick word with Mrs Funk to explain briefly?
- Well, Mrs Albrecht rang me this morning, and I was asked to call her back.
- My name is Jochen, Jochen Stäbel. We met at a conference in Amsterdam last week.
- It's Jule Funk. I'm phoning to check on the new design.
- It's with regard to placing an order.
- I'm phoning to request a schedule of rates and prices.
- I would like to offer some background information on ...
- I found your company on the Internet and I'd like some information about ...
- It's confidential.

**Vocabulary:**
check on: überprüfen
place an order: einen Auftrag erteilen
schedule of rates and prices: Preisverzeichnis

# Obtaining information

Using the telephone for obtaining information can be very useful, provided that the true purpose of such a call is information gathering and not selling. The three paragraphs below give example phrases for asking contact details, asking for the right contact and obtaining additional information.

## Contact details

- May I have his contact details, please?
- Could you give me the direct telephone number and fax-line please?
- I wanted to ask you some detailed address information.
- What's your full address / postal address?
- Just give me your PO box address please.
- What is the postal code / ZIP code please?
- Where is your company located?
- I'm afraid I didn't catch your name?
- What's the department manager's name?
- Would you be so kind as to give me Mr Fischer's e-mail address?
- Who have I been speaking to?

**Vocabulary:**
contact details: Kontaktdaten
direct telephone number: Telefondurchwahl
postal code / ZIP code 🇺🇸: Postleitzahl

## Asking for the right contact

- I was given your name by Mrs Funk.
- I would like to ask information on the latest software update. Who is dealing with this matter?
- We want to upgrade the European version. Which department is responsible for this?
- I'd like to speak to the person in charge of ..., but I don't know his or her name. Can you help me?
- Could you tell me who's responsible for the Austrian market, please?
- Who do I need to contact for information about ...?

## Obtaining additional information

- In addition, I would like to ask you for a valid price list.
- Could you send me a catalogue of your products?
- We would like to receive a copy of your terms of sale.
- How much is the annual turnover approximately?

**Vocabulary:**
upgrade: aktualisieren
catalogue / catalog 🇺🇸: Katalog
terms of sale: Verkaufsbedingungen

in addition: zusätzlich
annual turnover: Jahresumsatz

# I beg your pardon?

When communication doesn't go smoothly, or when you need a few seconds to switch over to another language, the following phrases may help:

## Technical problems

- Your line was busy 🇺🇸 / engaged 🇬🇧.
- I couldn't get through. / There was no reply.
- Sorry, I can't hear / understand you.
- Could you speak a little louder, please? The connection is quite bad.
- This connection is pretty bad, I can hardly hear you. Let me just hang up and call you back immediately, OK?
- Can you hear me alright?

## Language problems

- Could you speak a little slower please? I don't really speak English that well.
- Sorry, I didn't catch that. That was too fast for me.
- Could you repeat the last sentence once more, please?
- Would you mind saying that again?
- I'm sorry, I don't know that word. What does it mean?

- I'm very sorry. I don't understand. Could you explain that please?
- I can't understand you properly.
- Perhaps you could e-mail it to me, in case I didn't write it down correctly.
- May I connect you with someone who speaks English / German?
- Is there anyone in your office who speaks German?

## Wrong number

- Sorry, wrong number. Please, excuse my mistake.
- Oh, sorry to have bothered you. I must have gotten the wrong extension.
- I'm afraid you have the wrong connection.
- I'll put you through to the operator again, hold on.

**Vocabulary:**
the wrong connection: falsch verbunden
call the wrong number: sich verwählen

> Well, if I called the wrong number, then why did you answer the phone?
> James Thurber (1894 - 1961).

# Connecting people

Whenever you need to connect someone speaking English, or need to be connected yourself, there are many phrases to do so in a friendly and polite way. The examples below cover such situations as when a line is busy or when someone is not available.

### Please hold the line

- Hold the line, please. / Could you hold please? / Just a moment / minute, please.
- I'll put you through 🇬🇧/ I'll connect you 🇺🇸.
- It's ringing for you 🇬🇧.
- Putting you through to accounts now. / I'll connect you with the person in charge.
- I had best directly connect you with Mrs Neigel.
- Our specialist, Mr Fischer, can take your call now.

### Vocabulary:
person in charge: zuständiger Mitarbeiter
It's ringing for you: ich habe Sie durchgestellt
I had best directly connect you with ...: ich verbinde Sie am besten direkt mit ...

## Person not available

- I'm sorry, but he's on another call /on the other line at present. Would you like to hold or call back later?
- Mrs Funk is having a meeting and I can't disturb her. Can I connect you with her colleague Mr Lorentz?
- I'm afraid Mrs Hausner is not available at the moment. Can I pass you to her assistant / colleague?

## Person not in

- Mrs Heitz is not in at the moment. She said she would be back at eleven o'clock.
- Mr Fischer is in a meeting at the moment. Shall I try someone else for you?
- I'm sorry but Gisela is not in the office today.
- I'm sorry, but Jutta is no longer with the company.

## Asking when someone is available

- Do you know when she's free?
- When will he be available?
- When is the best time to reach her?
- Could you tell me what time she will be back?
- Could you try again, please?
- Has he got a deputy?
- Can I speak to his secretary?

**Vocabulary:**
deputy: Stellvertreter
suits: passt

# Answering the phone

When answering a business telephone call in English, it is common practice to start with a greeting, not to simply mention one's last name or company name. Receptionists will usually ask: 'How can I help you?' In private phone calls however, people might answer with just their telephone number or a simple 'hello'. Then the caller is expected to identify him or herself.

- Good morning. ABC Text & Redaktion.
- Tulip Technology. Good afternoon.
- Presseasy. Jule Funk here. How can I help you?
- Marketing Department. Julia here.
- Good morning. Andreas Obermaier speaking.

# Ending a conversation

It is important to close a conversation properly before saying 'good-bye'. By using phrases as in the following examples you are assured of a polite closing and you leave a good impression.

# Ending a conversation

## Example

A: It was nice talking to you, Mr. Murphy.
B: Yes, indeed. Well, I'll have my secretary schedule an appointment. And thanks again for the information.
A: You're welcome. Bye.

C: Could I contact you by e-mail?
D: Yes, let's keep in touch by e-mail.
C: Good. Well, thanks for taking the time to talk with me.
D: That's alright. Bye then.
C: Goodbye.

E: Well John, it's been nice talking to you.
F: Can I call you if I have any questions?
E: I'm very sorry, I have another call waiting.

## Pre-closing

One can't just launch into closing without a preamble. Here are some ways to introduce getting out of a conversation:

- Is there anything else I can help you with today?
- So, I think that's everything then?
- It was nice to make contact at last.
- Good to speak to you again.
- It's been nice talking to you. - Yes, nice to talk to you, too.

## Thanks for calling

- Thank you for phoning / calling (me) back / ringing.
- Thank you for getting back to me.
- Thank you for your time.
- OK, fine. Well, thanks, Mr Kauner.

## Thanks

Expressing thanks or appreciation in English is usually done with more adverbs or adjectives then one would expect.

- Thank you ever so much.
- I can't thank you enough.
- It's been most kind of you to help us.
- Thanks very much for your help.
- Thank you for the information.
- Many thanks.
- That's very kind of you.

## No thanks

After people have expressed thanks, it is customary to give a short equivalent of 'gern geschehen'. Any of the following phrases will do:

- You're welcome.
- Don't mention it.
- Pleasure.

- That's alright.
- Not at all. / No trouble at all.

## Follow up

Below are some phrases that give a call to (future) action:

- When can I expect to hear from you?
- Speak to you soon / next week then.
- Could I call you again in a week's time?
- That's agreed then, until Friday.
- I look forward to seeing you soon / hearing from you.

## Saying good-bye

Usually a simple 'bye' or 'good-bye' is enough, because a polite closing has been made in the phrases before. Below are examples of slightly different parting phrases:

- Alright. Bye then.
- Bye for now.
- Have a good weekend.
- Goodbye. And give my regards to Claudia.

## I'll have to stop

As mentioned elsewhere in this book, the British tend to communicate in a bit more indirect way. The examples below offer a decent way of ending a call with the proper respect.

- Can I phone you later, when I have some spare time?
- I'm sorry, but I really must get on now. I'll e-mail you a summary of the discussed point. Is that alright?
- I'm very sorry, but I must hang up now.
- I'll have to stop you there. I'm expecting a visitor.
- I'm sorry, I have another call waiting.

# Typical Situations and How To Deal with Them

One always has to deal with typical telephone situations. In order to cut a good figure this chapter explains to you:

- how to leave or make recorded messages (page 28),
- how to make appointments and arrangements by telephone (page 30),
- how to say names and telephone numbers, as well as e-mail and website addresses (page 38, 42, 45),
- how to leave voice mail or answering machine messages (page 49).

# Taking and leaving messages

When people are not available a message can still inform the other party. This does not only apply to your own phone, but also when answering someone else's phone. Therefore, don't forget to offer to take a message.

## Check-list: leaving messages

Good messages include information such as:

1 The date and time of the call
2 The name of the caller and/or company
3 Contact data of the person (if necessary) and what time they can be best reached by phone
4 The details of the call: question, problem, solution, proposal, follow-up, etc.
5 An indication which next steps you expect

## Taking messages

- Would you like to leave a message? / You can leave a message if you want. / May I take a message?
- Can I get him to call you back?
- May I take your name and number?
- No problem. I'll find a notepad. Hold on please. / Could you wait a minute?
- Let me just get a pen. Right, what's the message?

- Right, Kerstin, I'll make sure that he gets the message.
- Alright. I'll leave that on his desk. / Fine, I'll see that he gets that.

## Asking to leave a message

- I'd rather leave a message.
- Could I leave a message for Mr Ferdinand Ilahi please?
- Could you ask him to call me back? My number's 012-3456-789.
- Could you tell her that I will call back later, please?
- Could you please tell him Dr Schroeder called?

## Leaving specific messages

- Can she call me as soon as she gets in?
- Could you ask him to phone me on Tuesday afternoon?
- Yes, tell Romeo that Julia would like him to e-mail the confirmation before 5 o'clock tomorrow.
- Could he e-mail his report to me by Monday, please?
- I need her to phone me as soon as possible. My name's Kopfkaas, that's K-O-P-F-K-double A for Amsterdam-S.

**Vocabulary:** by Monday: spätestens bis Montag

## Responding to messages

- Thanks for your message about the postponement.
- Thanks for phoning back / calling me back, Peter.

- I'm just returning your call.
- I've just got your SMS / e-mail and I ...

# Appointments

The essence of making appointments is of course finding a convenient date and time for a meeting. Besides arranging the right moment, it might be practical to think about a realistic time period for the meeting in advance. The following example phrases can be used when making appointments.

## Examples

A: Hello Jochen, Klaus here. I'm calling about arranging a meeting with Moritz. Can you make Thursday after lunch; at three thirty?

B: Yes, that's fine.

A: Shall we meet in our office?

B: Yes, that seems a good idea.

A: Our office is on the second floor (US third floor). But just ask for me at the reception desk. I'll fax you a map.

B: That's very kind of you. Let me just confirm: Thursday the 25th, 3:30 at our office.

A: That's right. I look forward to it. Goodbye.

B: Bye.

A: Sorry for interrupting you again Jochen, but it's about the date we arranged for our meeting. I'm calling to fix another date because apparently Moritz is busy all week. Can we postpone it to Friday?

> B: I'm just looking at my diary. OK, here we are. Hm, I'm afraid I'm unavailable on Friday. What about Monday afternoon?
>
> A: Alright, I'll put that in my agenda. So that's Monday the 29th at 3.30. I'll confirm it by e-mail.
>
> B: Thank you.
>
> A: Not at all. Goodbye.
>
> B: Goodbye.

**Vocabulary:**
US third floor: im zweiten Stock
reception desk: Empfang
map: Wegbeschreibung
apparently: offenbar / anscheinend

## Introducing an appointment

- I'm calling to arrange / fix a time for that conference call with Munich.
- Could I make an appointment to see her sometime this week?
- I need to make an appointment with Mr Weischenberg as soon as possible.
- I've just spoken to Fabian and apparently he can attend the meeting next Monday at ten o'clock German time.
- Let's meet in the restaurant at a quarter past twelve.
- Hello S.M., Jule here. I just wanted to check the time of our meeting tomorrow.

**Vocabulary:**
fix a time: Zeit ausmachen
attend a meeting: an einer Besprechung teilnehmen

## Arranging an appointment

- Which day would be convenient for you? / Which day would you prefer?
- How about next Friday or the following Monday? / Are you free on Monday?
- What about Thursday instead?
- Would the morning / Monday afternoon suit you?
- Is two thirty OK?
- Anytime next Thursday sounds fine.
- I'm afraid I can't manage Monday.
- I've got another meeting at four thirty.
- Well, it won't take more than an hour.
- So that's Monday at three o'clock. / Monday at three is confirmed.

## Cancelling appointments

- I'd like to cancel / put off / postpone our appointment / interview.
- I am afraid I will not be able to keep the appointment I made for Friday, June 26th.
- I'm afraid I can't make it by 3 o'clock on Friday.

- Would it be possible to put off our meeting until tomorrow?
- I'm afraid Professor Krämer must change his appointment for the afternoon. Could we make another one?
- I'm sorry but an urgent matter has come up at the very last moment.
- I'm sorry but I haven't been able to get in touch with you before.

**Vocabulary:**

put off: verschieben
postpone: aufschieben
get in touch with you: Sie erreichen können

## Indicating date and time

When trying to arrange an appointment, pay attention to using the proper expressions concerning time and date. The fact is, that there are not only specific differences between German and English (e.g. the twelve-hour clock), but also some variations between British and American English. In case of doubt, always try to double check appointments or ask for confirmation by e-mail or fax. Electronic agendas like MS Outlook offer practical functions that automatically send reminders per e-mail.

## Months

| | | | |
|---|---|---|---|
| January | Januar | July | Juli |
| February | Februar | August | August |
| March | März | September | September |
| April | April | October | Oktober |
| May | Mai | November | November |
| June | Juni | December | Dezember |

## Dates

- 🇬🇧 26 June, reads as: 'the twenty-sixth of June'.
- 🇺🇸 June 26, reads as: 'June twenty-sixth'.
- 🇬🇧 26th June, reads as: 'June, the twenty-sixth'.
- 🇬🇧 2009, reads as: 'two thousand and nine'.
- 🇺🇸 2009, reads as: 'two thousand nine'.

Please note that years are usually pronounced in pairs: e.g. nineteen ninety-nine (1999).

## Ordinal numbers

1st - first
2nd - second
3rd - third
4th - fourth
5th - fifth
6th - sixth
7th - seventh
8th - eighth (only one 't')
9th - ninth (no 'e')
10th - tenth
11th - eleventh
12th - twelfth ('f' not 'v')
20th - twentieth
21st - twenty-first etc.

## Days

| | |
|---|---|
| Monday | Montag |
| Tuesday | Dienstag |
| Wednesday | Mittwoch |
| Thursday | Donnerstag |
| Friday | Freitag |
| Saturday | Samstag, Sonnabend |
| Sunday | Sonntag |

| | |
|---|---|
| today | heute |
| tomorrow | morgen |
| yesterday | gestern |
| the day before yesterday | vorgestern |
| the day after tomorrow | übermorgen |
| as from today 🇬🇧 / as of today 🇺🇸 | von heute an |
| this Thursday | diesen Donnerstag |
| next Tuesday | nächsten Dienstag |
| by Friday | bis Freitag |
| on Saturday | am Samstag, Sonnabend |
| a week on / from Monday | Montag in einer Woche |
| in a fortnight's time 🇬🇧 / in two weeks' time 🇺🇸 | in vierzehn Tagen |
| every Monday / on Mondays | jeden Montag, montags |
| in 6 days' time | in sechs Tagen |
| last / next month | im letzten / nächsten Monat |
| last week | letzte Woche |

## Times of the day

| | |
|---|---|
| in the morning | morgens, am Morgen |
| early morning | der frühe Morgen |
| morning | Morgen, Vormittag |
| midday | Mittag |
| lunchtime | Mittagszeit |
| before lunch | vor dem Mittag |
| after lunch | nach dem Mittag |
| in the afternoon | nachmittags, am Nachmittag |
| afternoon | Nachmittag |
| late afternoon | Spätnachmittag |
| evening | Abend |
| in the evening | abends, am Abend |
| in the morning | am Vormittag |

## What time?

In the United States, Canada (except Quebec), New Zealand and Australia, it is common to use the 12-hour clock (12-Stunden-Angabe), in which the day is divided into two periods called A.M. (ante meridiem) and P.M. (post meridiem). In most other countries the 24-hour notation is preferred. The list below also shows other ways of indicating the time.

# Appointments

Perception of time may differ from culture to culture. In the UK, for instance, people tend to give each other a margin of several minutes. The Irish saying 'When God created time, he created plenty of it' is of course only a generalisation; it nevertheless indicates that punctuality might be looked upon differently from country to country. Therefore, always plan telephone meetings with a sufficient margin because they may start a little bit later than expected.

| | |
|---|---|
| at 8 (o'clock) in the morning / 8 a.m. | um 08:00 Uhr |
| at 8 (o'clock) in the evening / 8 p.m. | um 20:00 Uhr |
| till 5 (o'clock) in the evening / 5 p.m. | bis 17:00 Uhr |
| after three (o'clock) | nach 15:00 Uhr |
| before three (o'clock) | vor 15:00 Uhr |
| as from 3 p.m. 🇬🇧 / as of 3 p.m. 🇺🇸 | ab 15:00 Uhr |
| between three and five (o'clock) | zwischen 15 und 17 Uhr |
| a quarter past nine | viertel nach neun |
| a quarter to nine | viertel vor neun |
| three thirty | halb vier |
| half eight 🇬🇧, (half past eight) | halb neun (not: halb acht!) |
| twenty-five minutes past ten | zehn Uhr fünfundzwanzig |
| five to twelve | fünf vor zwölf |
| noontime | Mittag |

| | |
|---|---|
| half an hour | eine halbe Stunde |
| quarter of an hour | eine Viertelstunde |
| three quarters of an hour | eine Dreiviertelstunde |

# Telephone spelling

When speaking in another language, it can sometimes be difficult spelling family or street names. That's why it is practical to develop a skill at spelling. Try to practice the pronunciation of all individual letters. It is also important to use the same spelling consistently, otherwise people might get confused. Tell callers in advance that you intend to spell a name. This gives them a chance to get a hold of pen and paper.

In the past, it was customary to first mention a letter, followed by 'as in' or 'for' and then a full word, but nowadays it is recommended not to use such phrases because they take more time and may even confuse a caller. Start spelling with an introduction phrase like: "The name is Bonn, James Bonn. I'll spell that for you: Berlin - Ottawa - double New York."

### Example

A: Can I have your name please?
B: That's Oxfoord.
A: Could you spell that please?
B: Oxfoord is spelt O-X-F-O-O-R-D.
A: Sorry, was that X for Xylophone?
B: Yes, that's correct, and then double O (or: Oliver Oliver).
A: I see. Thank you so much.

## Check-list: spelling

1 Notify your calling partner before you start spelling.
2 Pronounce the alphabet words quickly.
3 Try to avoid the use of phrases like 'for' or 'as in'.
4 It is not necessary for the other side to repeat each letter.
5 Many countries use a regional telephone alphabet.
6 Double letters are repeated in the US, but in the UK preceded by: 'double'.
7 The German 'e' sounds like the English 'a'.
8 In the US the 'z' is pronounced like [zii] and in the UK like [zed].

## Useful phrases

- I'm afraid I didn't catch the last name. Would you mind spelling it for me?
- Would you like me to spell the company name?
- Can you spell that using a telephonic key, please?
- Is that 'I' as in Italy, or 'E' as in Edison?
- Did I hear you correctly: MYER, not with EY, just with Y?
- I'd better read that back to you.

## Vocabulary:
catch: verstehen
spell: buchstabieren

telephonic 🇺🇸 key: Telefonbuchstabiertafel
read back: aufsagen

## Telephone alphabets

The following table shows the regional differences in spelling. You can use the British alphabet for countries of the Commonwealth. The American alphabet can be used in both the North and South American continent. For all other countries the international alphabet is recommended.

| Letter | English        | American | International |
|--------|----------------|----------|---------------|
|        | for, as in     | as in    |               |
| A      | Alfred         | Able     | Amsterdam     |
| B      | Benjamin       | Baker    | Berlin        |
| C      | Charles        | Charlie  | Casablanca    |
| D      | David          | Dog      | Denmark       |
| E      | Edward         | Easy     | Edison        |
| F      | Frederick      | Fox      | Florida       |
| G      | George         | George   | Greenland     |
| H      | Henry          | Harry    | Havana        |
| I      | Isaac          | Item     | Italia        |
| J      | John           | Jack     | Jerusalem     |
| K      | King           | King     | Kilogram      |
| L      | London         | London   | London        |
| M      | Mary           | Mary     | Madrid        |
| N      | Nellie         | Nancy    | New York      |
| O      | Oliver         | Oliver   | Ottawa        |
| P      | Peter          | Peter    | Paris         |

| | | | |
|---|---|---|---|
| Q | Queen | Queen | Quebec |
| R | Robert | Roger | Roma |
| S | Samuel | Sam | Sydney |
| T | Tommy | Tom | Tripoli |
| U | Uncle | Uncle | Upsala |
| V | Victoria | Victor | Valencia |
| W | William | William | Washington |
| X | Xylophone | X-ray | Xantippe |
| Y | Yellow | Yellow | Yokohama |
| Z | Zebra | Zebra | Zuerich |

## Pronunciation alphabet

| | | | | |
|---|---|---|---|---|
| A | ee | | N | en |
| B | bii | | O | oo |
| C | sii | | P | pii |
| D | dii | | Q | kju |
| E | ii | | R | ar |
| F | ef | | S | es |
| G | djii | | T | tii |
| H | eetsch | | U | ju |
| I | ai | | V | vii |
| J | dzjee | | W | dàbbel ju |
| K | kee | | X | eks |
| L | el | | Y | wai |
| M | em | | Z | zed 🇬🇧 / zii 🇺🇸 |

## Specific German letters

The umlaut is a specific German diacritic which looks like a dieresis (trema), or a pair of dots above a vowel. An umlaut is used for vowel mutation and can be replaced by an extra 'e' after the vowel. The German letter 'ß' (Eszett or scharfes s) can be replaced by a double 's'.

### Example

A: What was the address again?
B: That's Kantstraße number 5; the second last letter [ß] is called Eszett in German. But you can simply replace that with double 's'.
A: I understand, how interesting.
B: Thank you. Well, goodbye.
A: Bye.

**Vocabulary:** second last: vorletzter

# Taking down names and numbers

## Telephone numbers

Telephone numbers are much easier to understand, when pronounced in groups and divided by a pause. Therefore try to use single numbers when saying telephone numbers, and group them with pauses (e.g. 96-69 = 'nine six - six nine', not 'ninety-six sixty-nine'). However, prefixes or extensions of phone numbers are never grouped. Note that double numbers like 66 can be spoken as 'six - six' or 'double - six'. The number 0 is usually pronounced 'oh' or 'zero', never as 'nought'.

## Example

A: What's your phone / fax number?
B: 5678 9330 – five six seven eight [pause] nine double three oh.
A: Sorry, could you repeat the last part?
B: Yes, it's nine double three zero.
A: And what's your area code again?
B: 0-2-0, that's oh two oh, for London.

## Useful phrases

- Call me on 0123 456, or try my mobile: 987 654 321.
- What's the international code? / What's the country code?
- It might just be that fax numbers in Germany can have a variable length, sir.

### Vocabulary:
area code: Ortsvorwahl
international code: internationale Fernkennzahl
country code: Landeskennzahl

## Numbers on the phone

To pronounce numbers on the phone in another language can be harder than one would expect. In English the numbers after twenty have a different order then they do in German. For instance, einundzwanzig becomes twenty-one. Furthermore, the American 'billion' means 'Milliarde'. There are also some differences concerning the pronunciation of amounts or fractions. We just saw that there are different translations for the number '0' (null). But when pronouncing a telephone number, always use 'oh', as in: 'double oh, forty-nine' (00-49). In figures, however, it is better to use the word 'nought' 🇬🇧 or 'zero' 🇺🇸. For instance, 'an amount with six noughts / zeroes'.

## Decimals

Decimals are divided by either a comma or a point. The consequence of this is that amounts need to be pronounced with the word 'point'. For example, 0.2 is read as: nought (zero) point two, and the amounts in the examples below are all pronounced as: 'twenty point fifty euros' or 'twenty euros fifty'. By the way, note that the currency sign for Britain and Ireland is typed in front of the amount, and without a space.

## Example

United Kingdom: £20.50
Germany: 20,50 €
Ireland: €20.50

## Large numbers

100 - one hundred
200 - two hundred
101 - a hundred and one
900 - nine hundred
1,000 - a thousand
100,000 - a hundred thousand
1,000,000 - a million
1,000,000,000 - a billion (eine Milliarde!)
$10^{18}$ - 🇬🇧 trillion, 🇺🇸 quintillion - eine Trillion

In American English there is a tendency to pronounce figures like 180, as one hundred eighty. Whereas in British English, this is pronounced as one hundred *and* eighty.

## Fractions

½ - one half
¼ - one-quarter, one-fourth (ein Viertel)
⅓ - one-third
⅔ - two-thirds
1½ - one and a half

# Electronic addresses

Giving an electronic address in another language can be difficult. The main reason for this is that not everybody always knows the translations for unusual punctuation marks. As a matter of fact, the first programmers who designed electronic communication looked for the least used characters on a key-board. That was because in e-mail and Internet addresses it was impossible to use spaces. The following paragraph gives you an overview of all essential phrases and vocabulary you need to communicate an electronic address with ease.

## Digital vocabulary

| @ (at sign) | At-Zeichen / Klammeraffe |
|---|---|
| attachment | Anlage |
| back slash | umgekehrter Schrägstrich |
| dot | Punkt |

| e-mail | die E-Mail (D), das E-Mail (A, CH) |
|---|---|
| file | Datei |
| hard disk | Festplatte |
| hyphen | Bindestrich |
| slash | Schrägstrich |
| subject | Betrifft / Betreff |
| to | an |
| to download | herunterladen |
| to forward | weiterleiten |
| underscore | Unterstrich |
| wireless | drahtlos |

## Useful phrases

- What's your e-mail address?
- My e-mail address is: info@bfai.de. That's info at B for Berlin, F for Florida, A for Amsterdam and I for Italia, dot D-E.
- That's all lower case and no capitals.
- All details can be found on deutsche-boerse.com. That's DEUTSCHE with C-H-E, then a hyphen followed by BOERSE with O-E and ending with E for Edward, dot COM.
- The Internet address is: www.austria.gv.at/english. Please note that the address contains a second level domain. So there is a dot before and after G-V. Then it's dot A-T slash ENGLISH.

## Electronic country codes

People, who are used to electronic addresses ending with dot-de or dot-com, might have some difficulties with the type of addresses that use a second level domain (SLD). Usually such extra codes indicate an activity ('co' for companies, 'gov' for governments, etc.). Such an address contains an extra dot and the specific code. An example is: www.bbc.co.uk

In fact, quite a few countries use this type of electronic address. In addition to most Commonwealth countries and South America, countries like Austria, Sweden, Turkey or Japan, also use such URLs. When trying to locate a website, or writing down someone's e-mail address, it is practical to know the suffix of the country in question. The list below gives an overview for Anglophone countries. The country names are translated as well.

| Code | English | German |
|---|---|---|
| sld*.au | Australia | Australien |
| .ca | Canada | Kanada |
| sld.hk | Hong Kong | Hongkong |
| sld.in | India | Indien |
| .ie | Ireland | Irland |
| sld.nz | New Zealand | Neuseeland |
| sld.za | South Africa | Südafrika |
| sld.uk | United Kingdom | Großbritannien |
| .com | United States | Vereinigte Staaten |
| .gov | | |

**\* sld.** means second level domain: e.g.
http://www.airberlin.co.uk/

## Computer variations

The QWERTY keyboard layout of English-speaking countries differs somewhat from the QWERTZ layout in German-speaking countries. Not only are the Z and Y keys interchanged, but also the separate keys for characters such as ä, ö, ü or ß are missing. Furthermore, the function keys have different names or abbreviations.

The table below gives an overview:

| | |
|---|---|
| Ctrl (control) | Strg |
| Delete | Entf |
| Shift | Ums |
| Caps Lock | Umsch. Tastst |
| PgUp (page up) | Bild hoch |
| PgDn (page down) | Bild runter |
| Insert | Einfg |
| Home | Post |
| End | Ende |
| PrtSc (Print Screen) | Druck |

## Keyboard combinations

Sometimes it can be useful to give someone a so-called alt-code, allowing them to type a specific letter. The table below gives an overview for the most common letters.

| Letter | Alternative | Upper case | Lower casel |
|--------|-------------|------------|-------------|
| Ä | a e | Alt-142 | Alt-132 |
| Ö | o e | Alt-153 | Alt-148 |
| Ü | u e | Alt-154 | Alt-129 |
| ß | s s | Alt-225 | Alt-225 |

# Answering machine and voice mail

Although Willy Müller already invented the first automatic answering machines in 1935, many people still seem to hang up on recorded messages. Is it a fear of microphones or of disembodied voices? It probably hasn't been investigated yet, but one can imagine that people find it difficult to improvise while being taped, especially when it concerns leaving messages in a second language. The section below gives you examples for making your own recorded messages in English, as well as leaving messages.

## Check-list: leaving messages

1 Be prepared for voice mail: know in advance what to say.
2 A message contains six Ws: who, what, where, when, why, what way.
3 Write down some keywords or specific English vocabulary.
4 Always mention your first, last and company name; people may not recognise your voice due to technical reasons.

5 Specify the next steps: do you need to be called back?
6 Try to mention two different times at which you will be available.
7 Pronounce telephone or fax numbers slowly because who wants to listen to messages twice?

## Answering machines

- You are connected with the voice mail of Črt Perović. Please leave a message after the tone.
- You're connected with 12 34 56 78. Please leave a message after the tone.
- Welcome to Oberbilk Computing. Our offices are open from 9 to 12 and from 1 to 5.
- Hello, you're through to Oberbilk Computing. We are now closed for the holidays 🇬🇧 / vacation 🇺🇸 until August 21st. In an emergency call 0800 – 123 456. Thank you.
- Leave your message or send a fax after the tone.

## Private answering machines

- Hello, I'm afraid I'm not in at the moment. But please leave your name and phone number after the beep 🇬🇧 / bleep and I'll get back to you as soon as possible.
- Hello, this is Aynur. I'm sorry I cannot take your call right now, but if you'd like to leave your name and number, I will be happy to get back to you.

- Hello, this is Jack. I'm sorry, but there is currently no one here to take your call. Please leave a message. Or you can reach me on my cell phone at 1234 5678.

## Leaving a message

When leaving messages, it is important to speak slowly and clearly state your contact information. Despite all advances in technology it still is advisable to leave your telephone number, as not all international connections will indicate your caller ID.

- Hello, this is Claudia /my name's Claudia I work for ABC in Graz.
- This is a message for Julius Neigel. Could you please give me a ring tomorrow morning? I'll be in my office until 11. Thank you.
- I won't be in this afternoon but you can normally reach me between nine and twelve on 01-234, that's 01-234.
- My phone number is 1234 5678. Could you call me back, please? Thank you. I look forward to speaking to you. Goodbye.

> Try to talk slowly and clearly, because the sound quality of a reproduction is no more than 25% of the original.

## Recorded information

- If you want to speak to XYZ, press 1, for ABC, press 2, to speak to the operator press the star key (star button).
- To go back to the menu, please press the pound sign (hash key).
- Your call is being diverted to the voice mail service.
- The person you have called is unavailable. Please try again later.

### Example

Welcome to Oxford Summer Academy. If you require service in English, please press one. If you require service in German, please press two. For information on this month's summer academy please press three. If you wish to return to the main menu, please press four. If you are unsure of which option to choose, please hold and you will be connected to one of our operators as soon as possible. Thank you for calling Oxfoord.

# Mobile telephones

In most dictionaries you will have a hard time finding the specific words used in mobile telephony. The table below offers a selection of that terminology.

| | |
|---|---|
| cellular (phone), mobile (phone), cell phone | Handy, Mobiltelefon |
| network operator | Mobilfunkbetreiber, Mobilfunkanbieter |

| prepaid, Pay As You Go (PAYG) | Prepaidkarte, Guthabenkarte, Wertkarte (A) |
|---|---|
| ring tones | Klingeltöne, Töne |
| voice mail | Mailbox, Voicemail |

# Recognising mobile numbers

In many countries it is easy to recognise a mobile telephone number from the first digits. In the United States and Canada, however, mobile numbers cannot be recognised because they use the normal area codes. But since both outbound and received calls are being charged, the difference isn't so important from a cost point of view. The selection below allows you to verify whether a telephone number is a landline or not.

| Australia | 4 |
|---|---|
| Austria | 6 |
| Belgium | 4 |
| China | 13 |
| Cyprus | 99 |
| Czech Republic | 60, 72, 73, 77 |
| France | 6 |
| Gibraltar | 54, 58 |
| Hong Kong | 3, 6, 8, 9 |
| India | 9 |
| Ireland | 8 |
| Italy | 3 |

| | |
|---|---|
| Japan | 70, 80, 90 |
| Liechtenstein | 7 |
| Malta | 79, 99 |
| Netherlands | 6 |
| New Zealand | 21, 25, 27, 29 |
| Russia | 50, 51, 90, 91, 92 |
| Singapore | 8, 9 |
| South Africa | 7, 8 |
| Spain | 6 |
| Sweden | 7 |
| Switzerland | 76, 77, 78, 79 |
| United Kingdom | 7 |

# Special Situations

For those maintaining close connections with foreign business partners, it might sometimes be necessary to take part in more specific telephone calls.

In this chapter you will learn more about:

- how to make conference calls (page 56),
- how to make day-to-day business transactions by telephone – from ordering to negotiating contract terms (page 68),
- how to conduct a job interview by phone (page 87).

# Conference calls

Conference calls offer an alternative for travelling or overseas meetings because one doesn't have to go out of office for a particular meeting. Conference calls are becoming more and more popular, now that digital telephony (e.g. VoIP: Voice-over-IP) offers such cost-effective solutions. Combined with computer technology, it even allows us to share applications, making it possible to give a long-distance presentation, including the possibility to interact with the audience. Most conference calls, however, are still made by telephone. This can be done with a so-called group call, where several parties are phoned by an operator, or each party calls a specific telephone number and enters a pin code. For larger groups there are also special conference telephones. These are professional meeting telephones, with so-called duplex connections. Such machines ensure that the sound of all voices at a meeting table is at an understandable level.

## Practical tips

Non-verbal communication isn't possible over a telephone, therefore be careful with sarcastic or ambiguous remarks. Not everybody may recognise each other's voice. Therefore it is sometimes protocol to mention one's name before talking. This is also helpful for the person taking the minutes of the meeting. When you are attending a conference call, it is important that you understand key English phrases and expressions related to meetings. Also practical skills like keeping to the agenda, or knowing how to refocus, are components of an effective telephone meeting. This may sound simple in German, but it requires some preparation in another language. This paragraph will help you to hold or attend conference calls in English with success.

**Vocabulary:**
conference call: die Telefonkonferenz / das Sammelgespräch
agenda: die Tagesordnung
the chairman: die (der) Vorsitzende(r)
participant: der Teilnehmer

## Example

Good morning everybody, my name is Kevin Johnson, I'm the chairman of this conference call and I would like to welcome you all as participants to our telephone strategy meeting.

Let me start by reminding you that our call ends around 12 a.m. Also, I would like to inform you that the necessary conference documentation is called 'teleconf_report_3.doc' and that an audio recording of this conference call will be e-mailed to you as a mp3 file, together with a written summary. I will now quickly introduce you to all the other participants. May I ask you to greet the other members after your name is mentioned? This allows us to check that everyone is connected properly and that the technology is working smoothly. Thank you.

Then I would like, firstly, to welcome Mrs. Milena Albrecht from Munich, Germany. She will recapitulate the SWOT-and PEST analyses and will be available for questions. But that's item number three on our agenda. So let me first inform you of the sequence of today's discussion topics. As you can see from ... etc.

**Vocabulary:**
audio recording: Tonaufnahme
summary: Zusammenfassung

connected: angeschlossen
recapitulate: resümieren

## Welcome

To create a proper meeting atmosphere a chairperson welcomes the participants. In case new people join a conference, the welcome offers a good chance to introduce them to the other participants.

- Hello, everyone. Thank you for dialling in today. / First I'd like to welcome you all.
- Firstly, I want to thank you all for being punctual, despite this early hour for our colleagues from Washington.
- Thank you all for attending at such short notice.
- I know most of you, but there are a few unfamiliar 'voices'.
- As chair, it is my pleasure to introduce to you: Mrs Claudia Hausner. / I'd like to take a moment to introduce Claudia.
- You can request the help of our operator by using the hotkey *0.
- Well, since everyone is present, we should get started. / We have a lot to cover today, so we really should begin. / I declare the meeting opened / adjourned.

**Vocabulary:**
chair: Vorsitzende(r)
adjourn: schließen

## Absences

- The treasurer is absent due to unforeseen circumstances.
- Unfortunately, Jack cannot join us today, as he has been called away to Cologne.
- I have received apologies for absence from Julia, who is in London.

**Vocabulary:**
absence: Abwesenheit
unforeseen circumstances: unvorhergesehene Umstände

## Agenda

- Let me inform you of the sequence of discussion topics.
- There are six items on the agenda. First ..., second ..., third ..., lastly ... Shall we take these points in this order?
- Let's quickly go through the minutes from the previous meeting. Claudia, can I put you in charge of reviewing the minutes from the last meeting for us?
- Our agenda allocates ten minutes for this item, but I think ...
- Has everyone received a copy of the design proposal from Mrs. Cortez?
- But this matter is not on today's agenda.
- Well, the next item on our agenda is: questions and reminders.
- I think we've covered everything on the agenda.

## Chairperson

- Could I have your attention, please?
- I've called this meeting in order to ...
- I think we've spent enough time on this topic.
- I'm afraid we've strayed from the task at hand.
- I think we're steering off topic a bit with this.
- We've been arguing back and forth over this issue for some minutes now.
- It sounds like you've found some common ground; can you work that out bilaterally?
- We're running short on time. I suggest we skip the next item.
- We'll have to come back to this at a later time.
- I suggest that we address this matter again in our next conference call.

## Procedures

- If you have a comment, please introduce yourself by name, rather than simply speaking out.
- Peter, you may have the floor!
- Getting back to item number four, I'd like to propose ...
- I'd like to hand over to Julia Funk, who is going to lead the next point: marketing.
- As I mentioned in my opening remarks, we have to end this group call before the end of the hour.

- We'll have to keep each item to five minutes. Otherwise we'll never get through.
- We cannot speak all at once, please.
- Could you repeat that?
- If there are no further developments, I'd like to move on to today's topic.
- I suggest we go round the table.
- Jack, would you like to kick off?
- Gisela, would you like to introduce this item?

**Vocabulary:**
have the floor: das Wort ergreifen
go round the table: die Meinung aller Anwesenden einzeln einholen
kick off: anfangen

## Negotiations

### Example

A: Well, hello, everyone. My name is Horst, I am the Managing Director at the Paris office and I'm chairing today's meeting. We've organised this conference call to decide collectively by vote on Frankfurt's proposition. I hope you've all had a chance to look at Carsten's report. I suggest we go in the same order as last week's meeting and each say what we think, and afterwards we vote. Berndt, what is your opinion on the proposal?

B: Yes. Well, personally, I think the best solution is simply to wait. Despite Carsten's analyses.

C: Carsten here; I'd like to comment on that. I'm not sure I agree with that because as time passes the value also decreases.

> B: Well, in my opinion, that loss is not decreasing proportionately.
>
> C: I really think it would be better to act now, Berndt.
>
> A: We've been arguing back and forth for some minutes now, and we're running short on time. However, we'll have to come to a consensus here, so I suggest we put it to a vote now. Those of you in favour of the proposition please push the star key; all opposed, please push the pound key. Thank you.
>
> A: Gentlemen: the outcome of the vote is that the proposal has been adopted. Good, the next item on our agenda is: Berndt's report on outsourcing.

- We'd be willing to comply / agree with your counter proposal if you can reduce the insurance costs.
- The Berlin branch accepts a delay of one week, but that's their bottom line.
- We are very far apart on this issue.
- Shall we summarise the points of agreement?
- Do you accept these terms?
- I will send the proposal to you for your comments.

**Vocabulary:**

I'm chairing: ich präsidiere, sitze vor
decreasing proportionately: anteilmäßig abnehmend
comply: sich fügen in, einwilligen, nachkommen
counter proposal: Gegenvorschlag
branch: Niederlassung
bottom line: letztes Angebot
apart: auseinander
terms: Bedingungen
for your comments: zur Stellungnahme

## False friends

False friends are words that look similar, but mean something quite different in the other language. Below are some examples of German-English and English-German false friends.

| German | English | False friend | Translation |
|---|---|---|---|
| kontrollieren | to check | to control | beherrschen |
| Konzern | corporate group | concern | Belang |
| schließlich | eventually | eventuell | possibly |
| Streit | argument | Argument | point |
| wörtlich | literally | literarisch | literary |

## Personal opinion

It is important to realize that British tend to use polite expressions to take a strong stance. When you are taking part in a conference call, try to express yourself accordingly, and use one of the following phrases:

- I really think it would be better to ...
- The way I see things ... / From my perspective ... / Well, in our opinion, ...
- If you look at it from our point of view, then ...
- That's not exactly how I look at it.
- Well, personally, I think the best solution is ...
- I feel that ...

## Agreeing

The same indirectness as mentioned in the last paragraph applies to agreeing.

- I certainly agree to that. / I agree with you entirely.
- That sounds like a very good idea to me.
- We agree with you, as far as this is concerned.
- That's right / correct / possible.
- Can you agree to this proposal?
- We feel exactly the same way.
- We are agreed on this matter.

## Disagreeing

Telling another party that you disagree is usually softened with indirect elements as can be seen in the phrases below:

- We're not sure we agree with that.
- I'm afraid I'd have to disagree about that.
- That is not entirely correct.
- I'm afraid we cannot accept your statement.
- That's absolutely impossible / not possible.
- That's incorrect / not correct.
- The information seems insufficient / not accurate.
- I don't agree with that ...

## Providing feedback

- Mister / Madam chairman?
- Excuse me for interrupting, my name is ...
- I'd like to comment on that.
- Tom here, could I just say one thing?
- I'm glad you brought that up, Peter.

## Voting

- Since we cannot come to a consensus, I suggest we put it to a vote. All in favour please push the star key, all opposed can push the pound sign (hash key).
- The motion moved / suggested by Claudia is carried / agreed upon.
- There is a tie vote; I will therefore cast the deciding vote.
- I'll have Leonie Kootstra send out a group e-mail with the voting results.

**Vocabulary:**
pound sign / hash: Rautentaste
tie vote: Stimmengleichheit
deciding vote / casting vote: ausschlaggebende Stimme

## Closing / adjourning

As a chairman, one is responsible for the official closing of a telephone meeting. Use any of the following phrases:

- I just have a few closing remarks and then you will all be free to return to your desks.
- Before we close this meeting, let me just summarise the main items.
- If there are no further comments, we will adjourn the meeting here. Thanks for your participation.
- It looks like we've run out of time, so I guess we'll have to adjourn our conference call here.
- I'm afraid we're going to have to cut this meeting short.

## Final remarks

- Can we set the date for the next meeting, please?
- We'll meet again on the twenty-seventh of next month, same time. The minutes from today's meeting will be posted as of tomorrow morning.
- If anyone has any questions about what we discussed today, feel free to send me an e-mail. I neglected to mention that anyone who wants can receive a digital recording of this call.
- I'd like to thank Milena and Kevin for calling in from Amsterdam.
- Again, thank you all for taking time out of your busy schedules to be present.

# Hours for international business calls

What is the most convenient time to make conference calls with participants from different continents? The example table below shows the best possibilities, based upon German business hours. Because of the influences of daylight saving time, the times mentioned in August may differ from those in March.

| UTC | Friday 14 March | Thursday 14 August |
| --- | --- | --- |
| Berlin | Friday 17:00 | Thursday 17:00 * |
| London | Friday 16:00 | Thursday 16:00 * |
| New York | Friday 12:00 * | Thursday 11:00 * |
| San Francisco | Friday 09:00 * | Thursday 08:00 * |
| Chicago | Friday 11:00 * | Friday 10:00 * |
| Denver | Friday 10:00 * | Friday 09:00 * |
| Los Angeles | Friday 09:00 * | Friday 11:00 * |
| Hong Kong | Thursday 15:00 | Friday 14:00 |
| Sydney | Thursday 17:00 | Friday 17:00 * |
| Hobart | Thursday 17:00 | Friday 18:00 * |

* means the place observes daylight saving time (DST).

Know that certain countries (e.g. Thailand, Iceland etc.) or even states (e.g. Arizona) don't observe daylight saving time. A very practical website to compare international time zones is: www.timeanddate.com

**Vocabulary:**
Daylight Saving Time (DST): Sommerzeit
CET, Central European Time: MEZ, Mitteleuropäische Zeit
UTC, Coordinated Universal Time: Koordinierte Weltzeit

# International trade

This chapter is more directly concerned with tasks in the field of international trade. It discusses and illustrates how to tackle various everyday situations, such as enquiries, deliveries or legal matters. Besides containing many model phrases to suit your business needs, this chapter also informs you about idiomatic expressions and intercultural differences, in order to give you the best chance of communicating effectively.

## Example

A: Extension 213.
B: Hello, Mr Beer?
A: Yes, speaking.
B: Jolanda Bouman here.
A: Oh, yes, Mrs Bouman. How can I help you?
B: Well Mr Beer, I'm ringing to change our order number JB-07-03.
A: Can you refresh my memory and tell me what it was for?
B: It concerned that chicken delivery for October 1st.
A: Of course, I also see it on my computer now.
B: I would like to change the delivery date to October 8th if I may?
A: Naturally, but can I ask you to send me a note on that?

B: That's no problem. I'll fax it to you this afternoon.

A: That would be fine. In the meantime I'll arrange all necessary changes.

B: Thank you very much for your help.

A: Don't mention it. Bye for now.

B: Bye.

## Making enquiries

Below are some useful phrases for making an enquiry.

- We saw your stand at the Leipzig trade fair.
- I read about your firm in the trade press.
- Is your catalogue also available in German?
- Can you send me a copy of your catalogue and a price list?
- The prices you quote are without discount?
- Could I ask if you allow trial purchases?
- Can you supply from stock? I ask this because we require the goods by June 26 at the latest.
- The quality of the goods is of prime importance.
- Provided quality and price are satisfactory.
- The point is that we are working already at a reduced profit margin.
- We grant a discount of 69% on all catalogue prices.

**Vocabulary:**
enquiry: Anfrage
trade press: Fachpresse

trade fair: Messe
from stock: ab Lager
by ... at the latest: bis spätestens
provided: vorausgesetzt
quote: angeben
at a reduced profit margin: mit verringerter Gewinnspanne
grant a discount: Rabatt gewähren
trial purchase: Kauf mit Rücktrittsrecht / Kauf mit Option auf Rückgabe

## Ordering

- I placed an order with you this morning on the Internet and I'd like to change something. Who should I speak to?
- We'll get your order processed in the next few days.
- Could you please let me have some samples? It is rather urgent!
- Is there a discount for quantity?
- Please send us a note cancelling the initial order.
- Dominik Weischenberg here. I'm ringing to confirm receipt of our order number 2007/SR.
- Could your sales manager confirm this order in writing for us please?
- Would you confirm this conversation in writing please?

## Vocabulary:
confirm receipt: Empfang bestätigen
processed: erledigt
samples: Warenprobe

discount for quantity: Mengenrabatt
initial order: ursprünglicher Auftrag
sales manager: Verkaufsleiter
confirm in writing: schriftlich bestätigen

## Example

A: The Travel Company, Jill Smith speaking. How can I help you?
B: I should like to order a copy of "Paris City Guide" please.
A: Certainly sir, putting you through.
C: Good morning bookshop.
B: Hello, could I order one copy of "Paris City Guide" please?
C: Yes, of course, we have it in stock, so I can send out your order this afternoon.
B. That would be great.
C: Good, what name shall I put on the invoice, or do you perhaps have a customer number here?
B: Yes I do, it's 1001-MD.
C: Sorry, could you spell that?
B: One-double oh-one-M for Mary and D for David.
C: Thank you, anything else?
B. No, that will be all, thanks very much. Goodbye.
C: Goodbye Mrs Funk.

## Delivery

- Can you supply these products by June 26?
- I'd like some information about a shipment of boxes weighing 2,000 kilos each to New York City next week.
- You can send the goods directly to our premises in the Kantstraße in Berlin, carriage paid 🇬🇧 / freight prepaid 🇺🇸.

- May I ask who takes care of customs duties and insurance cover for this shipment?
- Who I should speak to about a delivery problem?
- Please let us know the current freight rate for sea / rail / air / road transport.
- What is the delivery time?
- I can promise you prompt delivery.
- Delivery may be delayed by 24 hours.
- When were the goods sent / dispatched?
- But I suppose the carrier issued a bill of lading?
- We'd like to know whether you can dispatch 1,999 books to Düsseldorf next Wednesday.
- We decided to send this consignment by general cargo.

**Vocabulary:**
by: bis zum
premises: Gebäude / Gelände
carriage paid: frachtfrei
freight prepaid: Fracht im Voraus bezahlt
customs duties: Zollgebühren
current freight rate: derzeitiger Frachtpreis
delivery time: Lieferfrist
prompt delivery: pünktliche Lieferung
delayed by 24 hours: um 24 Stunden verzögert
bill of lading: Konnossement
to dispatch: senden / schicken
general cargo: Stückgutladung

## Incoterms

The Incoterms 2000 (International Commercial Terms: Internationale Regeln für die Auslegung von Handelsklauseln) are a series of international sales terms which serve to divide transaction costs and responsibilities between buyer and seller. They are usually mentioned in an abbreviation-city combination (e.g. our prices are FOB Hamburg).

| Abbreviation | English | German |
|---|---|---|
| **Group E** | | |
| EXW | Ex Works | Ab Werk |
| **Group F** | | |
| FCA | Free Carrier | Frei Frachtführer |
| FAS | Free Alongside Ship | Frei Längsseite Schiff |
| FOB | Free On Board | Frei an Bord |
| **Group C** | | |
| CFR | Cost and Freight | Kosten und Fracht |
| CIF | Cost, Insurance and Freight | Kosten, Versicherung, Fracht |
| CPT | Carriage Paid To | Frachtfrei |
| CIP | Carriage and Insurance Paid To | Frachtfrei versichert |
| **Group D** | | |
| DAF | Delivered at Frontier | Geliefert Grenze |
| DES | Delivered Ex Ship | Geliefert ab Schiff |
| DEQ | Delivered Ex Quay | Geliefert ab Kai |

| | | |
|---|---|---|
| DDU | Delivered Duty Unpaid | Geliefert unverzollt |
| DDP | Delivered Duty Paid | Geliefert verzollt |

## Complaints

- I regret to have to complain about your consignment ...
- The goods delivered on the 27$^{th}$ of this month, were not the ones I had ordered.
- The goods that we ordered arrived damaged by water.
- Does your guarantee cover this damage?
- I must ask you to send a replacement as soon as possible.
- In accordance with the terms of the contract, I suggest ...
- We think you shouldn't have disregarded such a detail.
- I must point out to you, that the delay is causing us serious problems in the field of ...
- I believe a mistake has been made in invoice number 69C.

## Example

A: Good morning, AZ Werbeagentur. Can I help you?

B: Hello. Can you put me through to the service department, please?

A: Certainly. Putting you through now.

C: Service department, good morning.

B: Good morning, my name's Obermaier from Tulip Technology. I regret to have to complain. I rang last week about the fact that our customer database doesn't work properly, and I was promised full functionality by last Friday. However, we are still waiting for improvement.

C: I'm sorry Mr Obermaier, let me just check. ... It's due to circumstances beyond our control. But I'll see what I can do right now. Let me call you back by three o'clock, to let you know what the situation is.

B: Very well, three o'clock. But I must point out to you that this delay is causing us serious problems.

C: We are very sorry and I'll start calling right away to try and find a solution.

B: That would be fine. Thank you. Goodbye.

C: Goodbye, Mr Obermaier.

**Vocabulary:**

consignment: Sendung
replacement: Ersatz
terms of a contract: Vertragsbedingungen
disregard: missachten, nicht beachten

## Apologise

- I'm really sorry.
- We do apologise for the delay, but it's due to circumstances beyond our control.
- I'm afraid that we have made an error.
- I want to offer you an apology for this misunderstanding.
- Don't worry; we'll settle the matter as soon as possible.
- We are very sorry; apparently a mistake was made when the goods were shipped.
- I must admit that your complaint sounds totally justified.
- I must apologise again for the incorrect calculation of these costs.

- I must excuse myself on account of illness.
- I beg your pardon; I must have dialled a wrong number.

**Vocabulary:**
calculation of the costs: Kostenberechnung
on account of: auf Grund

## Legal matters

When referring to a contract or an agreement, it is important to use the right vocabulary. Legal language often has a specific meaning. The examples below also include some phrases in the field of international contract law.

### Example

A: Hello Klaus, I wanted to discuss a few details before entering into a contract.

B: Sure, Volkmar. So I understood.

A: It mainly concerns section 3, paragraph 4.

B: Yes, what about it?

A: It says here that unless we deliver within three working days, we are in breach of contract and the order can be cancelled.

B: That's part of our general agreements.

A: The point is we find three days very restrictive. Would you have a problem with one week?

B: No, under the circumstances that sounds fair. I'll have the changes made and e-mail you the draft contract this afternoon.

A: That's very kind of you Klaus. Thank you, and speak to you soon.

B: You're welcome. And give my regards to Rüdiger

- Shall I have Peter draft an outline agreement in the meantime?
- Naturally it is our intention to create legal relations.
- Can you have your lawyer prepare a written contract?
- ABC must simply fulfil 🇬🇧 / fulfill 🇺🇸 the obligations under the terms of the contract.
- Hamburg was deemed venue of jurisdiction in the case of disputes between the parties.
- But you did sign the invoice 'EOE' (errors and omissions excepted), if I'm not mistaken.
- Did the contracting parties agree on this particular forfeiture clause?
- We think that the shipping company has certainly not performed its contractual duties.
- We therefore claim that the deadline has been exceeded.
- The board specifically issued a power of attorney for me, to negotiate this matter.
- Our lawyer will file a lawsuit for breach of contract.

**Vocabulary:**

contracting parties: Vertragspartner
forfeiture clause: Verfallsklausel / Verwirkungsklausel
EOE / E & OE: Irrtümer und Auslassungen vorbehalten
venue: Gerichtsbezirk / Gerichtsstand
perform: erfüllen
exceed: überschreiten
terms of the contract: Vertragsbedingungen

power of attorney: Vollmacht
file a lawsuit: eine Klage einreichen
breach of contract: Vertragsverletzung

## Marketing

- Our marketing consultant is conducting a pilot survey.
- Will we have our normal modular stands available on the trade fair grounds?
- Does the stand rental also include all utilities and set-up?
- The report forecasts market leadership as of next year.
- Capturing a market share in Canada is the main objective.
- Sales have increased by 15% since we introduced more competitive pricing.
- We hope to maximise sales after this promotion scheme.
- Can your company cater to all potential customers in this market niche?

### Vocabulary:
trade fair: Handelsmesse / Fachmesse
set-up: Aufbau
pilot survey: Pilotumfrage
forecast: vorhersagen, voraussagen
capture market share: Marktanteil erobern
objective: Zielsetzung
competitive pricing: konkurrenzfähige Preise
promotion scheme: Werbekampagne
cater to: ausgerichtet oder eingestellt sein auf
market niche: Marktlücke

## False friends

False friends are words that look similar, but mean something quite different in the other language. Below are some examples of German-English and English-German false friends.

| German | English | False friend | Translation |
|---|---|---|---|
| Konzept | draft, plan | concept | Begriff, Idee |
| Konkurrenz | competition | concurrence | Einverständnis |
| Messe | fair; mass | mess | Unordnung |
| Bedeutung | meaning | Meinung | opinion |
| Marke | brand | mark | Note |
| Aktion | campaign | action | Handeln |
| Fotograf | photographer | photograph | Foto |
| Objektiv | camera lens | objective | Ziel |

# Sales and finances

## Selling a product or service

Making a telephone call with a potential customer is a difficult communication moment. However, with good preparation it may prove successful. Therefore prepare the right questions, listen as well as possible, and try to make notes during the conversation.

### Example

A: Could I ask you a few short questions?
B: What's it about?
A: It's about our brochure which we sent you last week. May I ask you what your initial reason was to ask for that information?
B: The main reason was to compare delivery times.
A: And why is this so important to you, Mrs. Funk?
B: Because we have to supply our customers.
A: I fully understand that's important to you. That's why I can propose to deliver all materials directly to your customers. In that way, I can even guarantee delivery within two days. Would that be a good solution for you?
B: Well, if you can actually guarantee that, it might.
A: Would you like me to send you some details per e-mail, or shall I show you some examples next week in your office?

- I would like to ask some short questions on ..., is that alright?
- We have branches throughout Europe.
- Our head office is located in Freiburg.
- It will only take about 14 minutes to see if we can help.
- I'll be in your area next week; could I make an appointment to see Mr Fischer on, say, Monday at 11 a.m.?
- What are the (dis)advantages of the present product, if I may ask?
- We provide free consultancy service for the duration of the contract, and our product is reasonably priced.

- I can offer you a discount of 5% off list prices. That is our final offer.
- Can you prepare a draft contract?
- So may I conclude that you accept our discount / payment terms?

**Vocabulary:**
branches: Filialen
head office: Hauptsitz
reasonably priced: preiswert
list prices: Listenpreise
draft contract: Vertragsentwurf
final offer: letztes Angebot
discount / payment terms: Rabatt / Zahlungsbedingungen

> A human being has two ears and only one mouth. Try speaking accordingly in sales calls: listen twice as much.

## Financial matters

International trade partly has to do with international finance. Recently some new financial vocabulary has been introduced. This paragraph illustrates various situations:

- I will need to mention your VAT number as well.
- I don't need the bank's number, but if you could give me your exact IBAN number and BIC code, please?
- Can you tell me where the nearest ATM (automated teller machine) is?

- Our portfolio manager makes day-to-day decisions about such investments.
- Did you receive a fax from us last week, reminding you about the outstanding account you have with us?
- I've been told by the accounts department that the invoice due on 27th November hasn't been settled yet.
- When was the bank transfer made?
- What are your usual terms of payment?
- Our trading partner demands a confirmed and irrevocable L/C (letter of credit).
- We offer a discount of 15% on orders exceeding 1,500 euros.
- These goods are paid in kind.
- I have instructed our bank to send a remittance every month.
- It's a standing order 🇬🇧, automatic transfer 🇺🇸.
- The point is: that price will be below our MSRP.

**Vocabulary:**
VAT (value-added tax) number: MwSt-Nummer
bank account number: Bankkontonummer
bank code number: Bankleitzahl
ATM: Geldautomat / Bankomat (A)
portfolio manager: Vermögensverwalter
outstanding account: unbezahlte / offenstehende Rechnung
accounts department: Buchhaltungsabteilung
due: verschuldet
settle: zahlen / begleichen

irrevocable: unwiderruflich
letter of credit: Akkreditiv
discount: Rabatt
remittance: Überweisung
in kind: Bezahlung in Naturalien / Sachspende
standing order / automatic transfer: Dauerauftrag
MSRP (manufacturer's suggested retail price): empfohlener Richtpreis
terms of payment: Zahlungsbedingungen

> **Bankleitzahl, IBAN and BIC**
> A 'BLZ' is called 'sort code' in the United Kingdom and Ireland, 'routing transit number' in the USA, 'bank transit number' in Canada, and 'BSB number' in Australia. This code or number serves to identify a branch of a bank for internal purposes. Nowadays specifying your **IBAN** account number (International Bank Account Number) is usually enough (China and the United States do not participate in IBAN at present). IBAN formats for the United Kingdom and the Republic of Ireland both use 22 characters. A **BIC** code (Bank Identifier Code) may also be called SWIFT address or SWIFT code.

# Travel enquiries

One often needs information about travel opportunities. The phrases in this section will help to plan when travelling.

## Hotel / conference

- I'd like to book a single room with a bath for Friday, 13th January please. / Do you have a double room with twin beds for three nights?

- Would you be so kind as to book a conference room accommodating 45 people?
- How much is that per day, please? / How much does it cost, please?
- How much is the charge for a second beamer, flip chart, white board?
- I'd like to rent a studio as from next October.
- What are your rates during the Frankfurt Book Fair?
- Can you recommend a hotel near your office?
- Could you let me have a confirmation by fax / e-mail?
- I have a reservation in the name of Anneke Hut.

**Vocabulary:**
as from: von ... an
in the name of: auf den Namen

### Example

A: Hello. The Ritz hotel, this is François speaking, how may I help you?
B: Hello, Julia Funk here, I'd like to book a room please.
A: Certainly, may I have your name again please?
B: That's Mrs Funk.
A: Sorry, could you spell that?
B: Funk: F-U-N-K.
A: Thank you, how many nights is that for?
B: Two, please.
A: When is it for, Mrs Funk?
B: October 3rd and 4th.
A: Would you like a single or a double room?

B: I'd like a double non-smoking room, please, as well as a conference room accommodating twelve people for October 4th.

A: May I ask for your credit card number to secure your reservation?

B: Yes, it is: Master 1234 567 8910.

A: And what is the expiry date?

B: It is October 2013.

A: Good, and could you give me a contact number Mrs Funk?

B: Yes, certainly my mobile number is 49-172 3456 789.

A: OK, I think that's everything. I have reserved a double non-smoking room for you on October 3rd and 4th, and a conference room for October 4th. Would you like a confirmation in writing perhaps?

B: No, that's alright, thanks.

A: Well, we look forward to having you here and hope you will enjoy your stay with us. Thank you, and goodbye.

B: Bye.

## Useful vocabulary

| American plan | Vollpension |
| --- | --- |
| B and B, bed and breakfast | Übernachtung mit Frühstück |
| double bed | Doppelbett / französisches Bett |
| double room | Doppelzimmer |
| full board | Vollpension |
| half board | Halbpension |
| high season | Hauptsaison |
| low / off season | Nachsaison / Vorsaison |
| king-size bed | 2-m breites Bett |

| queen-size bed 🇺🇸 | 1,5-m breites Bett |
|---|---|
| single room | Einzelzimmer |
| twin-bedded room | Zweibettzimmer |
| conference room | Konferenzraum |
| sound technique | Tontechnik |
| Internet access | Internetanschluß |
| secretarial support | Sekretariatsarbeiten |

## Restaurant

- I'd like to book a table for six for tonight, please.
- What time is that for exactly, sir?
- Do you also serve vegetarian dishes?
- What time does your kitchen close, if I may ask?
- Sorry, can I change the reservation for Ms Frist?

## Car rental

- I'd like to hire / rent a mid-range car, please.
- Is unlimited mileage included?
- How much is passenger insurance, comprehensive insurance or full insurance, please?
- Don't you have a manual / stick-shift available?
- I'd prefer to drive an automatic transmission.
- Do I have to pay a deposit?

**Vocabulary:**

mid-range car: Mittelklassewagen
unlimited mileage: uneingeschränkte Kilometerzahl
full insurance: Vollkasko

passenger accident insurance: Insassen-Unfallversicherung
automatic transmission: Automatikgetriebe

## Booking a flight

- I'd like to book a direct flight from Southampton to Düsseldorf on October 3rd please.
- Is there a connecting flight to Hamburg?
- Could you reserve an aisle / window seat, please?
- There are no domestic flights / internal flights available.
- I'd like to change my reservation on flight number 007.

**Vocabulary:**
connecting flight: Anschlussflug
change a reservation: eine Reservierung umbuchen
aisle / window seat: Gang- Fensterplatz
domestic / internal flight: Inlandflug

> single ticket 🇬🇧, one-way ticket 🇺🇸: einfache Fahrkarte
> return ticket 🇬🇧, round trip 🇺🇸: Rückfahrkarte

# A job interview by telephone

Nowadays, more and more North American companies employ phone interviews to save time and travel expenses. In this way, human resources managers or job recruiters actually use telephone interviews to narrow their selection of application letters. All too often, European job applicants aren't prepared for such job interviews by telephone. Try preparing for a phone interview just as you would for an in-person interview. Don't be afraid to use silence or an intentional pause when you need some time to think. Be prepared to give a quick description of your background, skills and knowledge. Always make sure that you have a copy of your résumé and cover letter at hand.

## Example

A: Good morning Mr Snorremans. I hope we are calling you at a convenient moment?

B: Yes, I expected your call.

A: First let me introduce you to Lynne Carter, who is listening on the other line.

B: Good morning. How do you Ms Carter.

A: Well, the first question I want to ask you is if you could tell us why you want this particular post?

B: As I wrote in my application, I'm very motivated to be a part of your new design team in Paris.

A: So, tell me about yourself Jorryt.

B: I'm currently senior designer for Jorritsma Controls which focuses on automotive and industrial design.

A: That's very interesting. We are considering inviting you to talk about the content and requirements of the position.

B: Can we schedule to meet in person over the next few days?

## About your curriculum vitae / résumé

- Could you describe your previous occupation, duties / tasks and the length of your experience?
- When did you encounter the greatest challenge of your career to date?
- I attended the University of Graz from 2001 to 2005.
- I graduated in the following subjects …
- I was promoted to department manager in 2007.

## About your current position

- I'm currently working as a … for X AG, focusing on …
- I am more interested in a full-time position. However, I would also consider a part-time position.
- My promotion prospects were limited in that company.
- I am looking for a similar position.
- I am looking for a position with more responsibility.
- I hope to improve my career prospects in your company.
- What's the salary range you're offering for the position?
- Let's talk about the content and requirements of the position first, so that we can better discuss compensation
- I want to thank you for the interview.

## When you are calling

- Good morning. Could you put me through to Human Resources, please?
- I'm calling in connection with your job advert in the Rheinische Post.
- It says I can get more information about the vacancy by calling this number.
- Good afternoon I'm calling about the job on your website.
- I have some questions about the content and requirements of the position.

**Vocabulary:**
curriculum vitae / résumé: Lebenslauf
letter of application / cover letter: Bewerbungsschreiben

## Questions to ask about a vacancy

- What are the day-to-day duties involved in this job?
- Why has this vacancy arisen?
- What challenges is the organisation currently facing?
- How quickly are you looking for someone?
- How will the performance be measured?
- Are you looking for anything in particular from the person who will fill the vacancy?
- What training and development possibilities exist for employees?

# Practical Reference

In this chapter you will find information on:

- dealing effectively with intercultural differences (page 92),
- the essential business terms for telephoning in English (page 100),
- the main linguistic differences between British and North American English (page 109).

# Intercultural communication

For successful international communication, just speaking the other language is not always enough. It is also necessary to have some basic understanding of the other culture. Certain behaviour is (also with respect to telephone calls) culturally defined, and misunderstandings can arise easily.

## Using names

For example, many English-speaking people will quickly be on first-name terms, whereas German-speaking people are more hesitant to mention their first names in a telephone conversation. Perhaps the reason lies in the fact that in the English language there is no difference between 'Sie' and 'Du', as they both are translated with 'you'. Another difference is that in the English language it is unusual for a man to call himself Mr Johnson on the telephone. For a woman, however, it's no problem to call herself Mrs Johnson, Miss Johnson or Cathy Johnson.

## Who identifies first?

In Britain it is not that uncommon to answer the phone by simply mentioning one's number or extension. For instance, 'extension 1013 speaking'. By the way, extension numbers are always pronounced digit by digit.

In many other cultures the telephone is answered in an impersonal way. Like the Italian 'pronto' (ready) or the Spanish 'dígame' (tell me). Their true function is only to let a caller know that the line is working and the caller can identify him or herself. It is simply a matter of different telephone etiquette.

## Directness

Intercultural studies by Hall, and more recently by Hofstede and Trompenaars, have shown that people from cultures like Germany, the United States, the Netherlands and Scandinavia have quite a direct way of communicating. People from Britain have a more indirect way of expressing ideas or feelings.

> Be aware not to express your wishes or criticism too directly when calling with people from more indirect cultures.

In order to communicate successfully, some knowledge of such culturally defined patterns seems necessary. It is certainly useful to mention the word 'please', in as many phrases as possible. On the other hand, certain German operators have been known to get irritated by the fact that not every Englishman always introduces himself when asking for an extension or a person. Effective intercultural skills probably imply that one has to accept certain differences.

In the business world, one has to deal with people and not with generalisations. Nevertheless, there are some generalisations worth keeping in mind. For instance, the fact that British tend to use more humour in business life. This is often seen as a professional opening to a conversation. On the other hand, British people don't like to show emotion, either in a business context or even in society in general. As a word of warning, it should be mentioned that there are also differences between the English, Scottish, Welsh, Northern Irish and Irish and that this can be quite a sensitive issue. Mixed feelings also exist about being part of the European Union, as essayist Richard Hill discovered when he heard the pilot say: ...'we're now leaving Europe, and the weather in Britain is fine'...

# Pronunciation

Although it can be very challenging for you to listen to someone speaking English over the telephone, some of us forget that listening to a non-native speaker may be even more difficult for the person on the other side of the line. Try, therefore, to pay attention to your weaker pronunciation areas.

### Emphasized syllables

Not every syllable is pronounced in English with the same force or strength. If you compare the words 'photograph', 'photographer' and 'photographic', they look very much alike when written, but when pronounced they actually sound quite different. This is because the accentuated syllable changes in each of the three words. Native speakers of English are used to concentrating on the accentuated syllables. If you are able to remember the right emphasis, people will understand you much better. The diagrams below help you to visualise the changes meant.

| Word pronunciation | Graphically | Number of syllables | Accentuated syllable |
|---|---|---|---|
| **PHO**-to-graph | | 3 | 1st |
| Pho-**TO**-graph-er | | 4 | 2nd |
| Pho-to-**GRAPH**-ic | | 4 | 3rd |

There are two simple rules that will help you remember accentuated syllables:

1 Each word has only one accentuated syllable.
2 Only vowels can be accentuated, not consonants.

## Tongue twisters

If you feel that you want to improve your pronunciation skills, try practising with the tongue twisters below. A tongue twister is a phrase that is difficult to pronounce correctly even for native English speakers, and are a popular form of wordplay. Try to say them as fast as possible, but correctly.

- Mixed biscuits, mixed biscuits.
- She sells sea shells on the seashore.
- Peter Piper picked a peck of pickled peppers.
- Around the rugged rocks the ragged rascals ran.
- We surely shall see the sun shine soon.
- I can think of six thin things and of six thick things too.
- Swan swam over the pond, swim swan swim.
- Three grey geese in green fields grazing.
- Cows graze in groves on grass which grows in grooves.
- Red leather, yellow leather, red leather, yellow leather.
- The sixth sick Sheik's sixth sheep is sick.
- A proper copper coffee pot.
- Comical economists.

**Vocabulary:**
tongue twisters: Zungenbrecher
word play: Wortspiel

# Speech

Intonation has been called the music in a person's voice. Or as the French saying goes: 'C'est le ton qui fait la musique'. And indeed, according to American psychologist Mehrabian, a good forty percent of our communication is influenced by the tone of our voice. This is, by the way, much lower than the fifty-five percent which is influenced by non-verbal communication, but then again; telephone calls aren't influenced by that. There are more elements besides intonation that can influence the way a phone call is perceived. We take a closer look below at: speed, volume, timing and articulation.

Professional telemarketers, for instance, try to talk slower on the phone, because people are then supposed to listen longer. The key to retaining a listener's attention is to also use clear, compact, fact-filled sentences when you speak. Try interjecting short responses like 'yes, I see', 'aha', 'that's interesting' etc., to show that you're engaged in the conversation. Timing is another effective skill in telemarketing: when a pause is made just before an important word or phrase, the impact is much greater. People who talk too loudly run the risk of making an aggressive impression. But people who talk too softly might sound hesitant, and this is also supposed to make listeners tired. Articulation: try to use your jaws, tongue, lips etc. to pronounce everything clearly. Especially when talking in another language, audibility is an important factor. It can be effective to ask a colleague to listen to your own calling style. Or even better, record a few telephone conversations in order to evaluate yourself.

## Homophones

Homophones are words that have the same sound but a different spelling and meaning. Especially for non-native speakers these can sometimes be difficult. Below is a selection of some relevant business homophones.

| | |
|---|---|
| aisle | isle |
| buy | by |
| cell | sell |
| cent | scent |
| complement | compliment |
| fair | fare |
| hole | whole |
| hour | our |
| know | no |
| meat | meet |
| principal | principle |
| profit | prophet |
| right | write |
| sight | site |
| some | sum |
| stationary | stationery |

# False friends

False friends (or faux amis) are pairs of words that look similar, but differ in meaning in two languages. As false friends are a problem for second-language speakers, the table below simultaneously compiles some common German-English as well as English-German false friends.

| German | English | False friend | Translation |
|---|---|---|---|
| auch | also | also | thus, therefore |
| Bedeutung | meaning | Meinung | opinion |
| bekommen | to get | to become | werden |
| Chefkoch | chef | Chef | head |
| Direktion | management | direction | Richtung |
| eigentlich | actual(ly) | aktuell | up-to-date |
| glatzköpfig | bald | bald | soon |
| Handy | mobile 🇬🇧, cell phone 🇺🇸 | handy | griffbereit, praktisch |
| ich werde | I will | Ich will | I would like to. |
| Konkurrenz | competition | concurrence | Einverständnis |
| kontrollieren | to check, to monitor | to control | beherrschen, steuern |
| Konzept | draft, plan | concept | Begriff, Idee |
| Konzern | corporate group | concern | Belang |
| Kunst | art | Art | manner, type |
| Manager | CEO | manager | Filialleiter |
| Marke | brand | mark | Note |
| Meer | sea | See | lake |
| Messe | fair; mass | mess | Unordnung |
| Personal | personnel | personal | persönlich |
| Richtung | direction | Direktion | management |
| schließlich | eventually | eventuell | possibly |
| schnell | fast | fast | almost |
| Sporthalle | gymnasium | Gymnasium | High School |
| Stadt | city | City | downtown |

| | | | |
|---|---|---|---|
| Streit | argument | Argument | point |
| Tat | act | Akt | nude |
| Unternehmer | entrepreneur | undertaker | Leichenbestatter |
| vertraut | familiar | familiär | informal |
| wenn | if | when | wann |
| werden | to become | bekommen | to receive |
| wörtlich | literally | literarisch | literary |

A special kind of false friend is the so-called Germish, also referred to as Denglisch or Engleutsch. It refers to English influenced by German linguistic interference. Below are two examples, in which the mistakes have been italicised (kursiv gedruckt) with an alternative mentioned in parentheses.

- What time shall we meet *us*? (not reflexive).
- We'd like to *control* the project outcome. (check).

# Telecommunications terminology

This paragraph contains specific telephone terms and words for use in a business context. It explains, for instance, how to ask someone for their fixed line number as well as other distinctive vocabulary, which often cannot be found in an ordinary dictionary.

| | |
|---|---|
| area code | Vorwahl |
| battery charger | Ladegerät |
| ex-directory 🇬🇧, unlisted 🇺🇸 | geheime Telefonnummer |

| | |
|---|---|
| be on hold | in der Warteschleife sein |
| call forwarding | Rufumleitung |
| cellular, mobile, cell phone | das Handy, das Mobiltelefon |
| collect call | R-Gespräch, Rück-Gespräch |
| conference call | Konferenzschaltung, Telefonkonferenz |
| dial | Wählscheibe |
| dial-direct number, STD number | Durchwahl(nummer) |
| emergency call | Notruf |
| landline, fixed line | Festnetz |
| international dialling code | Landeskennzahl |
| key lock | Tastensperre |
| key pad | Tastatur |
| pound sign, hash | Rautentaste, Rautenzeichen |
| receiver, handset | Hörer |
| redial | Wahlwiederholung |
| star key | Sterntaste, Sternchen |
| subscriber's number | Rufnummer |
| switchboard | Telefonzentrale, Vermittlungsstelle |
| telephone book / directory | Telefonbuch |
| telephone booth / box | Telefonzelle |
| text messages | Textmitteilungen, SMS |
| toll-free | gebührenfrei, zum Nulltarif |
| voice message | Sprachmeldung |
| Yellow Pages© | Gelbe Seiten, Branchenverzeichnis |

# Translated geographical names

A number of cities in German-speaking regions have different names in English. The list below helps to prevent misunderstandings during a telephone conversation.

| | |
|---|---|
| Bayern | Bavaria |
| Braunschweig | Brunswick |
| Franken | Franconia |
| Frankfurt am Main | Frankfort |
| Hannover | Hanover |
| Koblenz | Coblenz |
| Köln | Cologne |
| Luzern | Lucerne |
| München | Munich |
| Niedersachsen | Lower Saxony |
| Nordrhein | Westfalen |
| North Rhine | Westphalia |
| Nürnberg | Nuremberg |
| Preußen | Prussia |
| Rheinland | Pfalz |
| Rhineland | Palatinate |
| Ruhrgebiet | Ruhr River Valley |
| Sachsen | Saxony |
| Schwaben | Swabia |
| Steiermark | Styria |
| Thüringen | Thuringia |
| Tirol | Tyrol |
| Westfalen | Westphalia |
| Wien | Vienna |

# Key terms: the company

The following tables provide a quick reference source when trying to describe elements or divisions of a company;

## Departments / Abteilungen

| orders | Bestellungen |
|---|---|
| accounting | Buchhaltung |
| purchasing | Einkauf |
| finance department | Finanzabteilung |
| research and development, R&D | Forschung und Entwicklung, F&E |
| information technology | IT-Abteilung |
| customer service | Kundenberatung |
| after-sales service | Kundenbetreuung |
| warehouse | Lagerhalle |
| logistics | Logistik |
| marketing | Marketing |
| assembly | Montage |
| public relations, PR | Öffentlichkeitsarbeit |
| human resources, personnel department | Personalabteilung |
| production | Produktion |
| legal department | Rechtsabteilung |
| sales department | Verkaufabteilung |
| out-of-office sales | Verkaufs-Aussendienst |
| sales support | Verkaufs-Innendienst |
| sales management | Verkaufsleitung |

| despatch, dispatch | Versand |
|---|---|
| sales and distribution | Vertrieb |
| administration | Verwaltung |
| advertising department | Werbeabteilung |

## Company positions

| shop floor worker | Arbeiter/-in |
|---|---|
| assistant | Assistent/-in |
| staff | Belegschaft |
| office staff | Büropersonal |
| director | Direktor, leitender Angestellter |
| managing director, CEO | Generaldirektor/-in |
| manager | Manager/-in |
| personnel | Personal |
| management | Unternehmensleitung |
| vice president | Vizepräsident/-in |
| supervisor | Vorgesetzter |
| chairman | Vorsitzender |
| board of managers | Vorstand |

## Company divisions

| department, section | Abteilung |
|---|---|
| branch | Filiale, Niederlassung |
| business unit, division | Geschäftsbereich, Sparte |
| head office, headquarters | Hauptsitz, Zentrale |

| holding company | Holdinggesellschaft |
| --- | --- |
| parent company | Muttergesellschaft |
| subsidiary | Tochtergesellschaft |

## Types of companies

In many businesses the phone maybe answered with the company name together with suffixes like AG, GmbH etc. This paragraph gives an overview of the different abbreviations that are in use in the Anglophone world. Although the judicial systems are very different, it is still sometimes very handy to have some kind of comparison. Therefore a German equivalent has been added, if applicable.

| Abbr. | Country | Legal entity | Equivalent |
| --- | --- | --- | --- |
| Assocs. | USA | Associates | |
| (Edms.) Bpk. | RSA | Proprietary Limited (Afrikaans: Beperk) | GmbH |
| CC / BK | RSA | Close Corporation (Afrikaans: Beslote Korporasie) | |
| | UK | Company Limited by Guarantee | |
| | UK | Sole proprietorship, one-man business | EU |
| | UK | Unlimited Company | GmbH |
| Co. | USA | Company | |
| Corp. | USA | Corporation (see: Incorporated) | AG |
| Cpt | Irl | Cuideachta phoiblé theoranta (Public Limited Company) | AG |

| | | | |
|---|---|---|---|
| d/b/a | USA | Doing Business As. | EU |
| ELP | Bah | Exempted Limited Partnership. | |
| IBC | Bah | International Business Company | offshore |
| Inc | Can | Incorporated. Limited Liability | |
| Inc. | Aus | Incorporated Association | |
| Inc. | USA | Incorporated | AG |
| L.P. | USA | Limited Partnership | |
| LLC | USA | Limited Liability Company | |
| LLP | USA | Limited Liability Partnership | |
| LTD | Aus, India | Limited | GmbH |
| Ltd. | Can | Limited (Quebec: Limitée, Ltée) | GmbH |
| Ltd. | Nz, RSA | Limited | GmbH |
| Ltd. | UK | Private Limited Company | GmbH |
| (Pty.) Ltd. | RSA | Proprietary Limited | GmbH |
| N.A. | USA | National Association | für Banken |
| NT | Can | Intermediary | |
| P.C. | USA | Professional Corporation | |
| P/L or Pty. Ltd. | Aus | Proprietary Limited Company. | GmbH |
| PC Ltd | Aus | Public Company Limited by Shares | |

| | | | |
|---|---|---|---|
| PLC | Irl | Public Limited Company | AG |
| PLC | UK | Public Limited Company | AG |
| PrC | Irl | Private Company Limited by Shares | GmbH |
| Pty.Ltd. Pte.Ltd. | Various | Proprietary Limited company | GmbH |
| Pvt. Ltd. | India | Private Limited Company | GmbH |
| Teo | Irl | Teoranta | GmbH |

**Country abbreviations**
Aus: Australia; Bah: Bahamas; Can: Canada; Irl: Irland; NZ: New Zealand; RSA: South Africa; UK: Großbritannien; USA: Vereinigte Staaten.

**German abbreviations**
AG: Aktiengesellschaft; GmbH: Gesellschaft mit beschränkter Haftung; EU: Einzelunternehmen.

## Which abbreviation is from where?

| Abbreviation | Country |
|---|---|
| Co | United States, Taiwan. |
| Co Ltd | Ireland, Gibraltar, Hong Kong, other Asian countries. |
| Corp | United States, Asian countries. |
| LLC | United States. |
| LLP | United States. |
| Ltd | United Kingdom, Canada, Gibraltar, Hong Kong, Ireland, Malta, New Zealand, Singapore, United States (occasionally). |
| PC Ltd | Australia. |
| PLC, Plc, plc | United Kingdom, Cyprus, Ireland. |
| Pty Ltd | Australia, Hong Kong, South Africa. |
| Co | United States, Taiwan. |

# Linguistic differences: UK – USA

George Bernard Shaw once wrote that 'Britain and America are two countries divided by a common language'.

But although there are some differences in spelling conventions or vocabulary, only a few words really cause misunderstandings. An example of this is the expression 'to table a motion'. In the UK this means to place it on the agenda, while in the US it means exactly the opposite (to remove it from consideration). No idea how this is solved in bilateral meetings...

## Spelling differences

If we take a closer look at the spelling differences between British and American English, the examples in the table below show you some typical spelling conventions. Many nouns and adjectives are turned into verbs by adding -ize (standardize) in the US, and -ise in Britain. If in doubt, you can simply adjust the spell check on your computer.

| UK | US |
| --- | --- |
| authorise | authorize |
| litre, theatre, kilometre | liter, theater, kilometer |
| colour | color |
| catalogue | catalog |
| cheque | (bank) check |
| defence, offence | defense, offense |
| programme (except computer program) | program |

It is sometimes said that the longest word is the British English. As can be seen in:

| UK | US |
| --- | --- |
| -our (labour, colour) | -or (labor, color) |
| -ogue (catalogue) | -og (catalog) |
| -ll (dialled, traveller) | -l (dialed, traveler) |

But there are exceptions, for example: enrolment (UK), enrollment (US).

### Different words

Besides the differences in spelling mentioned above, sometimes simply different words are used. Some of the more common ones are listed in the table below (listed by German translation for convenience):

| British English | American English | Translation |
| --- | --- | --- |
| beep | bleep | Piepton |
| directory enquiries | directory assistance | Telefonauskunft |
| call box | phone booth | Telefonzelle |
| engaged | busy | besetzt (Telefon) |
| ex directory | unlisted | geheime Nummer |
| dialling tone | dial tone | Freizeichen |
| dialling code | area code | Vorwahl |
| chemist's | drugstore | Apotheke |
| number plate | license plate | Autonummernschild |
| banking account | bank account | Bankkonto |
| banknote | bill | Banknote |
| petrol | gas(oline) | Benzin |
| company | corporation | Betrieb |
| booking | reservation | Buchung |
| enquiry | inquiry | Erkundigung |
| driving licence | driver's license | Führerschein |
| autumn | fall | Herbst |

| | | |
|---|---|---|
| curriculum vitae | résumé, school transcript | Lebenslauf |
| bill | check | Rechnung |
| solicitor/barrister | attorney | Rechtsanwalt |
| booking | reservation | Reservierung |
| return ticket | round-trip ticket | Rückfahrkarte |
| at cost price | at cost | Selbstkostenpreis |
| inland revenue | duty income tax | Steuereinnahmen |
| transport | transportation | Transport |
| underground | subway | U-Bahn |
| subway | underpass | Unterführung |
| expiry date | expiration date | Verfallsdatum |
| let | hire | vermieten |
| fortnight | two weeks | vierzehn Tage |
| flat | apartment | Wohnung |

## Grammar differences

Some grammar differences are consistent between American and British:

| UK | US |
|---|---|
| look out of the window | look out the window |
| last Monday week | a week ago last Monday |
| talk to, meet | talk with, meet with |
| I have (already) eaten | I (already) ate |
| River Thames, River Avon | Hudson River, Mississippi River |
| to be in a team | to be on a team |
| I've gone | I went |

Apart from American and British, other well-known varieties of English are Australian, Canadian, South African and New Zealand. Countries such as India, Nigeria and the Philippines also have many English speakers.

> Contractions in British English are generally written without a full stop (e.g. Mr, Mrs and Ms). American English however usually uses a full stop (called period in North America): Mr., Mrs. and Ms.
>
> **Mr – British**
> **Mr. – American**

## Vocabulary:
contraction: Zusammenziehung
full stop 🇬🇧 / period 🇺🇸: Punkt

# Telephone sources on the Internet

The following list gives the Internet addresses for business telephone directories in Anglophone countries.

| | |
|---|---|
| Australia | www.whitepages.com.au |
| Canada | www.yellowpages.ca |
| | www.maplepages.com |
| Cyprus | www.cytayellowpages.com.cy |
| Gibraltar | www.gibyellow.gi |
| Hong Kong | www.yp.com.hk |
| | www.cwhkt.com |
| India | www.indiacom.com |
| Ireland | www.eircomphonebook.ie |
| | www.goldenpages.ie |
| Malta | www.yellowpages.com.mt |
| | www.maltacom.com |
| New Zealand | www.whitepages.co.nz |
| South Africa | www.phonebookonline.co.za |
| | www.easyinfo.co.za |
| United Kingdom | www.thephonebook.bt.com |
| | www.yell.com |
| United States | www.yellowpages.com |
| | www.att.com |
| | www.verizon.com |

# National telephone numbering plans

Calling another country is no longer simply a matter of leaving the first zero off the area code. Many countries have been changing their national numbering plans. Unfortunately, these changes were not always uniform. Certain countries, for instance, stopped using a zero completely, others stopped using area codes, and many countries now require area codes to be used for local calls (e.g. Switzerland, Spain, Denmark, Poland etc.). Some countries even created differences between international calls to a land line or to a mobile telephone. The company International Numbering Plans from Apeldoorn offers a free up-to-date database with specific details on its website: www.numberingplans.com.

In addition, the length of a number may vary: American phone numbers have a standard seven digits, very unlike German phone numbers which may have between three and eight digits. In other countries, mobile telephone numbers might have more digits than landline telephone numbers.

# Country codes and dialling codes for well-known cities

Use the table below for international country codes or the city dialling codes of English-speaking countries.

| Country / code | City code |
| --- | --- |
| Australia 00 61 | Adelaide 8, Albury 2, Brisbane 7, Cairns 7, Canberra 2, Darwin 8, Gold Coast 7, Hamilton 3, Hobart 3, Melbourne 3, Newcastle 2, Perth 8, Sydney 2. |
| Canada 00 1 | Alberta 403, British Columbia 250, British Columbia (Lower) 604, New Brunswick 506, Newfoundland 709, Nova Scotia 902, Ontario (London) 519, Ontario (Ottawa) 613, Ontario (Toronto Metro) 416, Ontario (Toronto vicinity) 905, Quebec (Montreal) 514, Quebec (Quebec City) 418, Quebec (Sherbrooke) 819. |
| Cyprus 00 357 | Famagusta 3, Kyrenia 357, Larnaca 4, Lefkonico 3, Limassol 5, Nicosia 2, Polis 6. |
| Gibraltar 00 350 | |
| Hong Kong 00 852 | |

| | |
|---|---|
| India<br>00 91 | Bengaluru (Bangalore) 80, Bhopal 755, Chennai (Madras) 44, Delhi 11, Hyderabad 40, Jaipur 141, Kolkata (Calcutta) 33, Mumbai (Bombay) 22, New Delhi 11, Pune (Poona) 212, Surat 261. |
| Ireland<br>00 353 | Cork 21, Donegal 77, Dublin 1, Galway 91, Killarney 64, Limerick 61, Sligo 71, Tipperary 62, Waterford 51. |
| New Zealand<br>00 64 | Auckland 9, Hamilton 7, Hastings 6, Invercargill 2, Nelson 3, New Plymouth 6, Tauranga 7, Wanganui 6, Wellington 4, Whangarei 9. |
| South Africa<br>00 27 | Bloemfontein 51, Cape Town 21, Durban 31, East London 431, Johannesburg 11, Pietermaritzburg 331, Port Elizabeth 41, Pretoria 12, Uitenhage 41, Welkom 57. |
| United Kingdom<br>00 44 | Aberdeen 1224, Belfast 2890, Birmingham 121, Blackpool 1253, Brighton 1273, Bristol 1272, Cambridge 1223, Cardiff 2920, Coventry 2476, Dover 1304, Dundee 1382, Edinburgh 131, Glasgow 141, Ipswich 1473, Jersey, Channel Islands 1534, Leeds 1532, Leicester 1533, Liverpool 151, London (city 207) (around 208), Londonderry 1504, Manchester 161, Newcastle 1632, Northampton 1604, Norwich 1603, Nottingham 191, Oxford 1865, Plymouth 1752, Portsmouth 2392, Sheffield 114, Southampton 2380. |

| | |
|---|---|
| United States of America<br>00 1 | Atlanta 404, Atlantic City 609, Austin 512, Baltimore 410, Boston 617, Cape Cod 508, Charlotte 704, Chicago 312, Cincinnati 513, Dallas 214, Denver 303, Detroit 313, Hawaii: 808, Hollywood 213, Houston 713, Indianapolis 317, Kansas City 816, Las Vegas 702, Long Beach 562, Los Angeles 213, Memphis 901, Miami 305, New Orleans 504, New York City (Bronx) 718, New York City (Brooklyn) 718, New York City (Manhattan) 212, New York City (Queens) 718, Palm Springs 760, Philadelphia 215, Phoenix 602, Pittsburgh 412, Salt Lake City 801, San Diego 619, San Francisco 415, Seattle 206, Washington 202, Yonkers 914. |

# Official holidays and translations

Finding the right translation for a national holiday during a conversation can be difficult. How would you explain *Mariä Himmelfahrt* or *Pfingsten* in English? But also when the other party isn't answering the phone, you might simply be calling during a local holiday. Below are English-German translations for the most commonly celebrated official holidays. Their specific dates can be found in the next paragraph:

| | |
|---|---|
| New Year's Day | Neujahr |
| Epiphany | Heilige Drei Könige |
| Carnival | Karneval / Fasching |
| Good Friday | Karfreitag |
| Easter | Ostern |
| Labour Day | Tag der Arbeit |
| Ascension Day | Christi Himmelfahrt |
| Whit Sunday | Pfingsten (Pfingstsonntag) |
| Whit Monday | Pfingstmontag |
| Corpus Christi | Fronleichnam |
| Midsummer's Day | Johannistag / Sommersonnenwende |
| Assumption | Mariä Himmelfahrt |
| All Saints' Day | Allerheiligen |
| Christmas Eve | Heiligabend |
| Christmas Day | Erster Weihnachtsfeiertag |
| Boxing Day | Zweiter Weihnachtsfeiertag |
| New Year's Eve | Silvester |
| National Day | Nationalfeiertag (auch für: Tag der deutschen Einheit) |
| Liberation Day | Tag der Befreiung |

## What are bank holidays?

A bank holiday is a public holiday in the United Kingdom and in the Republic of Ireland. Bank holidays are so called because they are the days upon which banks were closed by tradition (since the Bank Holidays Act of 1871). England and Wales share the same days, but Scotland, Northern Ireland and the Republic of Ireland all have their own public holiday.

# Country-specific holidays

Besides the commonly celebrated holidays, most countries have specific local public holidays.

## Australia

26 January - Australia Day, 25 April - ANZAC Day, second Monday in June - Queen's birthday

## Canada

24 May - Victoria Day, 1 July - Canada Day, first Monday in September - Labour Day, second Monday in October - Thanksgiving, 11 November - Remembrance Day

## England and Wales

7 May - May Day Bank Holiday, 28 May - Spring Bank Holiday, 27 August - Summer Bank Holiday

## Ireland

St. Patrick's Day, first Monday in May, June, August last Monday in October

## New Zealand

6 February - Waitangi Day, 25 April - ANZAC Day, first Monday in June - Queen's birthday, fourth Monday in October - Labour Day

## Northern Ireland

17 March - St Patrick's Day, 7 May - May Day Bank Holiday, 28 May - Spring Bank Holiday, 12 July - Orangeman's Day, 27 August - Summer Bank Holiday

## Scotland

2 January - 2 January, 7 May - May Day Bank Holiday, 28 May - Spring Bank Holiday, 6 August - Summer Bank Holiday, 30 November - St. Andrew's Day

## South Africa

21 March - Human Rights Day, 27 April - Freedom Day, 1 May - Workers' Day, 16 June - Youth Day, 9 August - National Women's Day, 24 September - Heritage Day, 16 December - Day of Reconciliation

## United States

Traditionally 30 May - Memorial Day, first Monday in September - Labor Day, 4 July - Independence Day - 4th Thursday in November - Thanksgiving Day

# Temperature conversion table

| Fahrenheit (°F) | Celsius (°C) |
| --- | --- |
| 212 (boiling point) | 100 (Siedepunkt) |
| 176 | 80 |
| 122 | 50 |
| 104 | 40 |
| 98.4 (body temperature) | 37 (Körpertemperatur) |
| 68 | 20 |
| 50 | 10 |
| 32 (freezing point) | 0 (Gefrierpunkt) |
| 14 | -10 |
| 0 | -17,8 |
| -459.67 (absolute zero) | -273,15 (absoluter Nullpunkt) |

**Conversion of Celsius and Fahrenheit:**

- °F – °C: (°F – 32) x 5/9 = °C
- °C – °F: °C x 9/5 + 32 = °F

# Weights and measures

| Weights | Gewichte |
|---|---|
| gross weight | Bruttogewicht |
| net weight | Nettogewicht |
| 1 ounce (oz) | 28,35 g |
| 1 pound (lb) | 453,6 g |
| 1 stone | 6,356 kg |
| 1 short hundredweight (cwt) | 45,359 kg (USA) |
| 1 long hundredweight (cwt) | 50,802 kg (GB) |
| 1 short ton (tn) | 907 kg (USA) |
| 1 long ton (tn) | 1016 kg (GB) |
| 1 metric ton | 1000 kg |
| **Linear measures** | **Längenmaße** |
| 1 inch (in) | 2,54 cm |
| 1 foot (ft) | 30,48 cm (12 in) |
| 1 yard (yd) | 91,44 cm (3 ft) |
| 1 mile (m) | 1,609 km (1760 yd) |

# Index

abbreviations 108
advance preparation 6
agenda 59
answering machines 50
answering the phone 22
appointments 30
beginning a call 7
companies, types of 105
company positions 104
complaints 74
conference calls 56
connecting people 20
country codes 116
dates 34
departments 103
differences UK-USA 109
directness 93
electronic addresses 45
enquiries 69
false friends 63, 79, 98
holidays 118
Incoterms 73
indicating date and time 33
introducing yourself 10
job interview 87
legal matters 76
marketing 78
measures 123
messages 28, 49
mobile telephones 52
names 10, 92
negotiations 61
numbers 34, 42
obtaining information 16
ordering 70
personal opinion 63
pronunciation 94
pronunciation alphabet 41
reason for your call 13
sales and finances 79
small talk 14
speech 97
spelling 39
telecommunications terminology 100
telephone alphabets 40
telephone scripts 8
telephone sources 114
temperature 122
thanks 24
time 36
times of the day 36
travel enquiries 83
weights 123

**Bibliografische Information der Deutschen Bibliothek**
Die Deutsche Bibliothek verzeichnet diese Publikation in der Deutschen Nationalbibliografie; detaillierte bibliografische Daten sind im Internet über http://dnb.ddb.de abrufbar.

ISBN 978-3-448- 08627-0
Bestell-Nr. 00967-0001

© 2008, Rudolf Haufe Verlag GmbH & Co. KG, Niederlassung Planegg b. München
Postanschrift: Postfach, 82142 Planegg
Hausanschrift: Fraunhoferstraße 5, 82152 Planegg
Fon (0 89) 8 95 17-0, Fax (0 89) 8 95 17-2 50
E-Mail: online@haufe.de
Internet: www.haufe.de
Redaktion: Jürgen Fischer

Alle Rechte, auch die des auszugsweisen Nachdrucks, der fotomechanischen Wiedergabe (einschließlich Mikrokopie) sowie der Auswertung durch Datenbanken oder ähnliche Einrichtungen vorbehalten.

**Gesamtbetreuung:** Sylvia Rein, 81371 München
**Lektorat:** Otto von Dehn, 46348 Raesfeld; Sylvia Rein, 81371 München
**Umschlaggestaltung:** Simone Kienle, 70182 Stuttgart
**Umschlagentwurf:** Agentur Buttgereit & Heidenreich, 45721 Haltern am See

**Druck:** freiburger graphische betriebe, 79108 Freiburg

# Der Autor

**Sander M. Schroevers**

arbeitet als Berater im Bereich der internationalen Kommunikation und PR. Er spricht häufig auf internationalen Konferenzen und hat bereits zahlreiche Bücher auf dem Feld der europäischen Kommunikation publiziert. Daneben ist er Präsident des IECIE-Gremiums, des Europäischen Instituts für Internationale Unternehmenskommunikation (L'Institut européen de communication internationale d'entreprise) in Paris.

# Weitere Literatur

„Business English: Small Talk", von Lisa Förster, 200 Seiten, mit CD-ROM, € 16,80, ISBN 978-3-448-08630-0, Bestell-Nr. 01058-0001

„Die besten Bewerbungsmuster Englisch", von Lisa Förster, 156 Seiten, mit CD-ROM, € 19,80
ISBN 978-3-448-06784-2, Bestell-Nr. 04078-0002

„Controlling-Fachbegriffe Deutsch-Englisch, Englisch-Deutsch", von Anette Bosewitz, mit CD-ROM, € 29,80
ISBN 978-3-448-06030-0, Bestell-Nr. 01418-0001

# TaschenGuides – Qualität entscheidet

Bereits erschienen:

- **Der Betrieb in Zahlen**
  - 400 € Mini-Jobs
  - Balanced Scorecard
  - Betriebswirtschaftliche Formelsammlung
  - Bilanzen lesen
  - Buchführung
  - Businessplan
  - BWL Grundwissen
  - BWL – die 100 wichtigsten Fakten
  - Controllinginstrumente
  - Deckungsbeitragsrechnung
  - Einnahmen-Überschussrechnung
  - Finanz- und Liquiditätsplanung
  - Die GmbH
  - IFRS
  - Kaufmännisches Rechnen
  - Kennzahlen
  - Kleines Lexikon Rechnungswesen
  - Kontieren und buchen
  - Kostenrechnung
  - Kleine mathematische Formelsammlung

- **Mitarbeiter führen**
  - Besprechungen
  - Führungstechniken
  - Die häufigsten Managementfehler
  - Management
  - Managementbegriffe
  - Mitarbeitergespräche
  - Moderation
  - Motivation
  - Projektmanagement
  - Spiele für Workshops und Seminare
  - Teams führen

- **Karriere**
  - Assessment Center
  - Existenzgründung
  - Ich-AG – mit Gründerzuschuss selbstständig
  - Jobsuche und Bewerbung
  - Vorstellungsgespräche

- **Geld und Specials**
  - Sichere Altersvorsorge
  - IGeL – Medizinische Zusatzleistungen
  - Immobilien erwerben
  - Immobilienfinanzierung
  - Die neue Rechtschreibung
  - Eher in Rente
  - Web 2.0
  - Zitate für Beruf und Karriere
  - Zitate für besondere Anlässe

- **Persönliche Fähigkeiten**
  - Allgemeinwissen Schnelltest
  - Ihre Ausstrahlung
  - Business-Knigge – die 100 wichtigsten Benimmregeln
  - Mit Druck richtig umgehen
  - Emotionale Intelligenz
  - Entscheidungen treffen
  - Fitness für Beruf und Karriere
  - Gedächtnistraining
  - Glück!
  - IQ-Tests
  - Knigge für Beruf und Karriere
  - Knigge fürs Ausland
  - Kreativitätstechniken
  - Manipulationstechniken
  - Mind Mapping
  - Nein sagen
  - NLP
  - Schneller lesen
  - Selbstmanagement
  - Sich durchsetzen
  - Soft Skills
  - Stress ade
  - Verhandeln
  - Yoga für Beruf und privat
  - Zeitmanagement